W9-AQN-738

Creative Dramatics in the Classroom

CREATIVE DRAMATICS IN THE CLASSROOM

BY NELLIE McCASLIN

Director, Mills Children's Theatre Workshop
Mills College of Education in New York City

David McKay Company, Inc.
New York

CREATIVE DRAMATICS IN THE CLASSROOM

LIBRARY OF CONGRESS CATALOG CARD NUMBER: 68–19636
MANUFACTURED IN THE UNITED STATES OF AMERICA

To

MARGARET M. DEVINE,

whose educational philosophy and quality of leadership have contributed so significantly to my own thinking as well as the point of view expressed in this book.

ACKNOWLEDGMENTS

We are grateful to the following for permission to reprint copyright material:

Mrs. Alice Ellison Brain, "Sing a Song of Seasons" by Alice Ellison; Albert E. Clarke, III, "Little Scarecrow Boy" by Margaret Wise Brown; E. P. Dutton & Co., Inc., "Jump or Jiggle" by Evelyn Beyer from *Another Here and Now Story Book* by Lucy Sprague Miller, © 1937 by E. P. Dutton & Co., Inc., renewal © 1965 by Lucy Sprague Miller; the estate of Dorothy Baruch Miller, "Merry-Go-Round" from *I Like Machinery* by Dorothy Baruch; Harper & Row, Publishers, Inc., "Halloween" by Geraldine Brain Siks from *Children's Literature for Dramatization* by Geraldine Brain Siks, © 1964 by Geraldine Brain Siks; the Literary Trustees of Walter de la Mare and the Society of Authors as their representative, "Some One" by Walter de la Mare.

We have been unable to trace the copyright owner of "Imaginings" by J. Paget-Fredericks and would welcome any information that would enable us to do so.

Foreword

While each chapter of Dr. McCaslin's book deals with a different aspect of "Creative Dramatics in the Classroom," they all converge in the single purpose of providing a new dimension for learning, one which appeals to all children and almost without exception results in a positive response.

The level of writing of this book is a practical one, but it also involves thorough insight into learning. This necessitates proven knowledge as well as sound theories, both of which are activated here through common sense and a happy anticipatory feeling that creative dramatics is something we might all enjoy together.

Adults interested in the development of children often lack the necessary understanding of how children learn, and what they are interested in, and how to put these two together. The few people who do know, and who are sound practitioners in their respective fields, seldom take the time to pass on to others their knowledge.

Dr. McCaslin's book will help many teachers as well as parents, students, and camp workers. Her emphasis on the seriousness of play, in the emotional and intellectual development of children, is most timely.

Unquestionably, Dr. McCaslin is deeply concerned with the development of the child's self-image through identification with other people and with characters in stories or poetry. This concern is reflected throughout the book, as she points out that all children need these opportunities. I was particularly pleased to find that creative dramatics was also urged for those deprived children who need it in order to breathe a bit of fresh air through a feeling of achievement, a gain in self-confidence, and in the simple beauty of expressing their own ideas freely.

From the experience of watching this author over a decade,

actively doing the things she writes about, I realize how her work has been able to influence, positively, the lives of many young people who are planning to be teachers. Needless to say, it has been a privilege to know and to work with Dr. McCaslin. I can only hope that some of her own delightful humor and imagination, and her faith in the soundness and ability of youth, may have rubbed off on me.

AMY HOSTLER, President Emeritus
Mills College of Education

August 8, 1967

Preface

This book has been written in response to questions and discussions with teachers and students regarding the inclusion of creative dramatics in classrooms, camp programs, and community centers. Some of the questions have arisen in college classes; more have come from participants in drama workshops. It is both interesting and heartening to note that workshops in creative dramatics are being offered in increasing numbers throughout the country each year under a wide variety of sponsorships.

Some of these workshops consist of a single session. Others are planned as a series, including as few as three meetings to all-day sessions over a period of one to three weeks. There is, of course, a variety of in-service classes for teachers, conducted along academic lines, which may be organized to include participation, demonstration, discussion, and the opportunity for wide reading in the field. More often, however, I have found the creative dramatics inclusion to be one unit of study in a course covering formal theatre techniques and speech activities. The pattern varies, as it should, according to the needs, demands, and time involved, as well as the availability and individual background of the leader.

It has been the experience of the author that the majority of those who enroll in such workshops, or classes, have had little or no previous training. All are eager to learn, but many express feelings of insecurity, often despite years of successful classroom teaching. Frequently-asked questions are: "What exactly is creative dramatics?" "How does one start?" "Where should it be introduced?" "What material is available?" "Don't you need a background in theatre arts?"

The questions are legitimate, and the author is most sympathetic. She is also aware, however, that the great majority of those who question their qualifications have the primary requisites: the desire to learn, a respect for the contribution of children, and an appreciation of the theatre arts. Without these basic attitudes, it is doubtful whether satisfying results can ever be achieved; with them, there is a likelihood of success.

Few teachers or students have had sufficient experience in the theatre arts to feel secure in the beginning. On the other hand, many who have studied formal theatre techniques have had no experience with creative dramatics. There is little doubt that the creative teacher will find his own way sooner or later, but if the following chapters suggest a point of view and a way of working, they will have served their purpose.

There are a number of excellent books now available in the area of both creative dramatics and children's theatre, and this book in no way purports to repeat what has already been written well and in considerable detail. What is intended here is a simple guide for the inexperienced leader or classroom teacher—the non-specialist—who wishes to initiate dramatic activities but who needs some practical help in getting started.

This book has, therefore, been conceived from a point of view rather than organized along specific age or class levels. Its very brevity would preclude a comprehensive treatment of the interests and expectations for each grade. Moreover, the author believes the philosophy, values, and techniques to be essentially the same for all, regardless of the age or grade level of the participants. Her own experience with teachers has convinced her that they are well aware of the interests, tastes, and backgrounds of their pupils. What they are seeking is guidance in the planning of simple exercises, and in the adaptation of material for use in creative dramatics. With this in mind, therefore, the following chapters have been planned so as to touch upon the questions many teachers ask.

The contents include a rationale for creative dramatics with specific objectives and values, exercises in pantomime, improvisation, play structure, and the simple basic procedures involved in preparing a play for an audience. While this is not intended to be a book on play production, the author knows that occasionally a group may wish to share its work with an audience, and when this happens, new problems are posed. Suggestions for solving the problems are not meant to encourage the practice but rather to help in making an easy transition from the purely informal exercise to the formal presentation.

It is hoped that the reader will also avail himself of the resources listed in the bibliography. Familiarity with the literature in the field will not only help him to build a better background but may, indeed, strengthen his own perception and awareness. He will then begin to create his own techniques, geared not to an arbitrary age or grade level, but, rather, to his own particular circumstances.

At this time I should also like to acknowledge the inspiration which has come from such leaders as Winifred Ward, Geraldine Brain Siks, Grace Stanistreet, Isabelle Burger, Agnes Haaga, and Muriel Sharon. Their philosophy and work have helped to shape my own views and their writing on the subject has contributed significantly to the field. My thanks go to those teachers who have raised questions which I am attempting to answer. Their desire to learn has stimulated my own thinking. And, finally, the college students and children, whom I have had the pleasure of teaching over the years, have demonstrated by their response the importance of an art which is as rewarding to the leader as it is to the group.

NELLIE MCCASLIN

Table of Contents

Creative Dramatics in the Classroom

CHAPTER 1

By Way of Introduction

PLAY

In every human being there exists the impulse to mime and to play. Primitive societies released this impulse through tribal expressions of hope, joy, fear, desire, sorrow, hatred, and worship. What primitive man felt strongly, he danced or mimed. From his sacred play came ritual; poetry, music, and dance were a part of his play. Philosophy and wisdom found expression in words.

In ancient Greece religious celebration resulted in contests, and these contests gave birth to dramatic forms or plays. As highly organized as they were later to become, these contests could be considered the creative expression of the people, from whose ranks individual playwrights emerged. During the Middle Ages, drama had its rebirth in the Church. Authorship of the scripts is unknown but there is proof that the performers were amateurs, whose participation was voluntary. Professionalism had no part in these plays, which served a religious and educational purpose. The involvement of the audiences was probably great as they responded to the dramatization of the Bible stories and moral tales as enacted by their neighbors. In every period of history, play has served a significant purpose, interpreting and affecting the lives of the people. "We have to concede, therefore, that civilization is, in its earliest phases, played." [1]

According to the author of this statement, our modern adult preoccupation with making a business of play has resulted in its decline, and this decline is man's loss. True play does not know professionalism, for it is a voluntary activity, based on, but different from the business of everyday life. Joy and freedom are the

---

1. J. Huizinga, *Homo Ludens, A Study of the Play Element in Culture* (Boston: The Beacon Press, 1955), p. 14.

hallmarks of play, with the rules and limits established by the players.

True play, though free, creates order—indeed, *is* order. Whereas man may play alone, one of the basic characteristics of play is the teamwork involved; through play, the participants are drawn closely together. Huizinga notes that dressing up is often an element of play, though it is not always included and is not necessary. Examples of play may be found in all countries of the world, at different periods in history and on every age level. Play is inherent in man, and the child early manifests an impulse to engage in it.

One has only to watch a group of children playing in an empty lot or on a playground to accept the truth of these observations. The child plays almost as soon as he moves, and through his playing, he learns. In his dramatic play the three- or four-year-old tries on the roles of those about him; he observes their activities and learns by pretending to be and do. He enters the various worlds of his family and neighbors, interpreting and reenacting. First he observes; then he responds. Not unlike primitive man, the young child expresses his feeling through movement and words, creating more complex situations as he grows older, with the boundaries stretched but the rules still clearly established. By the time he is ready for school he has learned much about the world he lives in, and a large part of his learning has come about through his play. As Winifred Ward has observed, "Drama comes in the door of every school with the child." [2]

The impulse to play, if encouraged, can become a continuing way of learning, a medium of expression, and eventually a creative art. Many teachers have realized the potential of play and have made drama an integral part of their programs. Some have rejected it on the grounds that it is frivolous and therefore unrelated to serious learning. The fact that the child gives it his most serious attention escapes their notice; he is made to feel that play is unworthy and therefore something to be left outside the schoolroom door. When this happens, the joyful and creative element of his free play

---

2. Winifred Ward, *Drama With and For Children* (Washington: U. S. Department of Health, Education and Welfare, Bulletin #30, 1960), p. 1.

is extinguished, perhaps never to be rekindled. Other teachers, and it is to them that this book is addressed, ask how they can keep the play impulse alive, that it may enhance learning and thus enrich the lives of their pupils.

EDUCATIONAL OBJECTIVES

One of the most frequently stated aims of education today is the maximum growth of the child both as an individual and as a member of society. In order to achieve this aim, certain educational objectives have been set up. Although these objectives vary somewhat, there is general agreement that knowledge, skills, and appreciation of the arts are essential. The modern curriculum tries to provide for each child to:

1. Develop basic skills in which reading, writing, arithmetic, science, social studies, and the arts are stressed
2. Develop and maintain good physical and mental health
3. Grow in his ability to think
4. Clarify his values and verbalize his beliefs and hopes
5. Develop an understanding of beauty, using many media including words, color, sound, and movement
6. Grow creatively and thus experience his own creative powers.[3]

Although other objectives are mentioned, these six are most frequently listed in the building of programs designed for today's world and the complex problems life offers.

The most enthusiastic proponent of creative dramatics would not go so far as to claim that its inclusion in the curriculum will ensure the meeting of these objectives. On the other hand, many of the objectives of modern education and creative dramatics are unquestionably shared. Among the shared objectives are:

(1) Creativity and aesthetic development
(2) The ability to think critically
(3) Social growth and the ability to work cooperatively with others

---

3. Robert S. Fleming, *Curriculum for Today's Boys and Girls* (Columbus, Ohio: Charles E. Merrill Books, Inc., 1963), p. 10.

(4) Improved communication skills
(5) The development of moral and spiritual values.

Before discussing creative dramatics in greater detail, definitions are in order. The terms, creative dramatics, playmaking, children's theatre, dramatic play, and role-playing, are used, often interchangeably, though they have quite different meanings. A definition of terms will clarify the meanings as they are used in this text.

DEFINITIONS

Dramatic Play

This is the free play of the very young child in which he explores his universe, imitating the actions and character traits of those around him. It is his earliest expression in dramatic form but must not be confused with drama or interpreted as performance. Dramatic play is fragmentary in nature, existing only for the moment. It may last for a few minutes or go on for some time. It may even be played repeatedly, if the interest is sufficiently strong, but when this occurs, the repetition is in no sense a rehearsal. It is, rather, the repeating of a creative experience for the pure joy of doing it. It has no beginning and no end, and no development in the dramatic sense.

Dramatic play may be as simple as Susan's passing of imaginary cookies to a guest when her mother is entertaining a friend at tea. The two or three minutes of spontaneous pantomime are indeed dramatic play since they involve stepping into the role of the mother and performing an often observed activity. Susan has seen how a hostess behaves, and is taking advantage of an opportunity to slip into the role to see what it is like to be "mother" and do as she does.

Dramatic play may, on the other hand, follow the pattern of six-year-old Erma, who was the youngest child on the street and, therefore, the last to go to school. She had heard about teachers and lessons, and longed for the day when she, too, could pack up her books in a bag and trot off after breakfast with the other boys and girls to the elementary school. When the time came, her curiosity may have been satisfied but her fascination became even more intense. According to her family, she would return every afternoon and set up her own class in the dining room. Whether the others joined her or not, she would play for an hour or more with an improvised desk and a blackboard. She assumed, in turn, the various roles of principal, teacher, boys and girls. Most often, however, she would be the teacher who called the roll, disciplined the children, and, to the great amusement of her mother and older sister, reenacted everything that had taken place during the day. This situation held her interest for three years, though the content varied according to her daily experiences. Other parents have described similar preoccupations, some lasting for an extraordinarily long time, until the interest waned and another took its place.

It has been stated that "dramatic play helps the child develop from a purely egocentric being into a person capable of sharing and of give and take." [4] Certainly this is true of the two examples cited. In both instances the mother accepted the play without interference, letting it continue with neither impatience nor the kind of amused attention that might have caused self-consciousness. In the book, *Understanding Children's Play,* the authors observe that through this activity the child is given an opportunity to imitate adults, encouraged to play out real life roles with intensity, to dramatize relationships and experiences, to express his own most pressing needs, to release impulses which are unacceptable, to reverse the roles usually taken, to try to solve problems and to experiment with solutions. If encouraged, by providing the place, the equipment, and an atmosphere in which the child feels free to express himself, dramatic play is a natural and healthy manifestation of human growth.

Creative Dramatics and Playmaking

These terms may be used interchangeably since they refer to informal drama which is created by the participants. As the name, "playmaking," implies, it goes beyond dramatic play in scope and

4. Ruth Hartley, Lawrence K. Frank and Robert M. Goldenson, *Understanding Children's Play* (New York: Columbia University Press, 1964), p. 19.

intent. It makes use of a story with a beginning, a middle, and an end. It is, however, always improvised drama. Dialogue is created by the players, whether the content is taken from a well-known story or is an original plot. Lines are not written down or memorized. With each playing, the story becomes more detailed and better organized, but it remains extemporaneous in nature and is at no time designed for an audience.

The re-playing of scenes is different from the rehearsal of a formal play, in that each member of the group is given an opportunity to play various parts; therefore, no matter how many times the story is played, it is done for the purpose of deepening understandings and strengthening the performers rather than perfecting a product. Scenery and costumes have no place in creative dramatics, although an occasional property or piece of a costume may be permitted to stimulate the imagination. When these are used, they should not be considered mounting, or suggest production. Most groups do not feel the need of properties of any kind, and are generally freer without them.

Whereas the term "creative dramatics" is used to describe the improvised drama of children from age five or six and older, it belongs to no particular level, and may be used just as appropriately to describe the improvisation of high school students. The young adult is more likely to label it "improvisation," which, indeed, it is, but the important distinction to keep in mind is that it has form and is, therefore, more structured than dramatic play. At the same time, it is participant-centered and not intended for sharing, except with the members of the group who are not playing and are, therefore, observers rather than audience.

Children's Theatre

The term, "children's theatre," refers to formal productions for children's audiences, whether acted by amateurs or professionals, children or adults, or a combination of both. It is directed rather than guided; dialogue is memorized, and scenery and costumes usually play an important part. Since it is audience-centered, it is essentially different from creative dramatics and dramatic play.

The child in the audience is the spectator and the benefits he derives, aesthetic.

What does a child gain from attending good children's theatre? He gains much. First of all, there is the thrill of watching a well-loved story come alive on a stage. There is the opportunity for a strong, vicarious experience as he identifies with characters who are brave, steadfast, noble, loyal, beautiful. Emotions are released as he shares the adventure and excitement of the plot. And, finally, he learns to appreciate the art of the theatre if the production is tasteful and well done.

We are speaking now of the child in the audience, not the child in the play. While there is much that is creative and of value for the performer, it is generally agreed that participation in creative dramatics is far more beneficial than public performances, for all children up to the age of eleven or twelve. Occasionally, there is an expressed desire "to put on a play," and when this comes from the children themselves, it is probably wise to grant the request. There are times, to be sure, when sharing is a joy and a growing experience but it is to be hoped that such occasions are infrequent. Certainly, if it is done, the production should be simple and all precautions taken to guard against the competition and tension that so often characterize the formal presentation of a play. For high school or college students, however, a play is often the desired culmination of a semester's work. To deprive students of the experience would be to withhold the ultimate satisfaction of communicating an art.

There are some leaders in the field who believe that any performance in front of an audience is harmful because it automatically interferes with the child's own free expression. The author would agree up to a point, but the theatre is, after all, a performing art, and when the audience is composed of understanding and sympathetic persons, such as parents, or members of another class, it may be the first step toward communicating a joyful experience. Without question, however, younger children should not perform publicly. Those in the middle and upper grades may not be harmed if their desire, and the right occasion, indicate that the benefits outweigh the disadvantages.

Role-Playing

This term is most often used in connection with therapy, or education. It refers to the assuming of a role for the particular value it may have to the participant, rather than the development of an art. Although all art may be considered to have certain curative powers, it is not the primary purpose of either creative dramatics, or theatre, to provide therapy or make use of drama to solve social and emotional problems. Role-playing is what the young child does in his dramatic play, it is true, but it is also a tool used by psychologists and play therapists.

Drama therapy is similar to role-playing in its stated purpose. Its use assumes a problem, for which this type of treatment is indicated. Physically handicapped, mentally retarded, emotionally disturbed, and culturally disadvantaged children may derive great benefit from its use, provided the therapy is in the hands of a competent and sensitive therapist. The distinction between role-playing and therapy, therefore, consists more of degree than of kind. *Role-playing* may be considered preventive, in that it provides an opportunity for all children in a group to develop sensitivity toward the feelings of others, and encourages changes of attitude through understanding. *Therapy* is the dramatic technique used for its curative power in helping a patient to solve problems which frighten, confuse, or puzzle him. "It is in itself both a form of comfort and reassurance, and a way of moving on toward new attitudes about these things." [5]

Creative Drama

This is the play that is developed creatively by a group, as opposed to the one that abides by a written script. When the dialogue is written by either teacher or children, it automatically ceases to be spontaneous drama, although it may, indeed, be a fine example of creative writing. This occasionally happens, and when it does,

---

5. Peter Slade, *Child Drama* (London: University of London Press, 1954), p. 119.

the results may be doubly rewarding. The play may be simple or elaborate, but if it is to be properly described as creative drama, it must be improvised rather than written.

Integrated Project

Frequently, several subjects in the curriculum are drawn together, with drama as the means of uniting them. Social studies, science, literature, dance, music, arts and crafts may contribute themes from which a play or pageant is fashioned. The integrated project is an effective way of stimulating interest, and illuminating subject matter. The only danger inherent in the practice lies in making dramatics a handmaiden to the other subjects. When this occurs, it does a disservice to both drama and to the material which it has tried to sugar-coat. We have all seen plays in which children were cast as foreign countries, vegetables, abstract qualities, even vitamins! It is highly questionable whether they have really learned anything about the subject presented; it is certain that they have missed the satisfaction of getting into a part with believable human qualities. When well done, however, an integrated project can be an exciting and creative way of learning, through which both subject matter and drama are well served.

VALUES IN CREATIVE PLAYING

There is general agreement among teachers of creative dramatics that important values can be gained from creative playing. Depending upon the age of the children, the particular situation, and the orientation of the leader, these values may be listed in varying order. It is the contention of this book, however, that in spite of these differences, certain values exist in some measure for all, regardless of age, circumstances, or previous experience. To be sure, the activities must be planned with the group in mind, and the emphasis placed upon the needs and interests of those involved. Whereas the five-or six-year-old needs and enjoys the freedom of large movement and much physical activity, this is not to deny a similar opportunity to boys and girls much older. Adult students in early sessions gain freedom and pleasure when given an opportunity to move freely in space.

The eleven-or twelve-year-old enjoys the challenge of characterization, and often creates with remarkable insight and understanding. The young child, however, can also create on his level, though he cannot be expected to compete with children who are older. In other words, it is not a question of assigning different values to various age levels; it is a matter of accepting basic values that exist on all levels, varying more in degree than in kind. Specifically, these values may be listed as follows:

An Opportunity to Develop the Imagination

Imagination is the beginning. In order to work creatively, it is necessary, first of all, to push beyond the boundaries of the here and now, to project oneself into another situation, or into the life of another person. Few activities have greater potential for developing the imagination than playmaking. Little children move easily into a world of make believe; but as we grow older, this amazing human capacity is often ignored, or even discouraged. The development of the imagination to the point where the student responds spontaneously may take time, in some cases, but it is the first step toward satisfying participation.

The sensitive teacher will not demand too much in the beginning, but will accept with enthusiasm the first attempts of the beginner to use his imagination to solve a problem. Once the player has had the fun of seeing, hearing, feeling, touching, tasting, or smelling something that is not there, he will find that his capacity grows quickly. Holding the image until he can do something about it is the next step, but the image must come first. Through drama, the imagination can be stimulated and strengthened to the student's everlasting pleasure and profit.

An Opportunity for Independent Thinking

A particular value of creative playing is the opportunity it offers for independent thinking and planning. Although the drama, both informal and formal, is a group art, it is composed of the contributions of each individual, and every contribution is important. As the group plans together, each member is encouraged to express his own ideas and thereby contribute to the whole. The leader recognizes the part each child plays, and the value that planning has for him. If the group is not too large, there will be many opportunities before the activity is exhausted. Thinking is involved in such questions as: "Who are the characters?" "What are they like?" "What part do they play?" "Why do they behave as they do?" "What scenes are important?" "Why?" "How can we suggest this action or that place?"

The evaluation that follows is as important as the planning: indeed, it is preparation for a re-playing. Children of all ages are remarkably perceptive, and their critical comments indicate the extent of their involvement. A well-planned session in creative dramatics provides exercises in critical thinking as well as an opportunity for creativity.

Freedom for the Group to Develop Its Own Ideas

It has just been stated that through creative dramatics an individual has a chance to develop and grow. This is also true of the group, in which ideas are explored, evaluated, changed, and used. As a group of any age works together under sensitive and skilled leadership, the members learn to accept, appreciate, and stimulate each other. Every teacher has experienced a group in which the dynamics were such that all seemed to produce more because of their association. This is not to say that creative dramatics is a magic formula for successful teamwork, but it unquestionably offers a rare opportunity for sharing ideas and solving problems together. The formal play, whatever problems it may pose, cannot offer a group this same challenge. The written script imposes a structure in which free improvisation has no place. There are values in formal production, to be sure, but the major emphasis is on the product, rather than on the participants.

The strength, incidentally, that is acquired through this kind of planning and playing together is a valuable asset, when, at some later date, the group decides to give a formal play. Far from limiting the players, improvisation strengthens techniques and builds individual and group rapport.

An Opportunity for Cooperation

When a group builds something together, it is learning a valuable lesson in cooperation. Social differences may be forgotten in the business of sharing ideas and improvising scenes. Teachers who guide children in creative dramatics cite numerous examples of social acceptance based on respect for a job well done, and the bond that develops from the fun of playing together. As an illustration, Jack entered a neighborhood class in dramatics, which several of his third-grade schoolmates attended. It was obvious that he was an outsider, and the leader despaired of his ever becoming a part of the group. For the first three or four sessions, he contributed nothing and was chosen by no one, regardless of the activity.

Then one day the children were dramatizing the story of *The Stone in the Road*. They wanted a farmer, to drive along the road with a donkey cart. Several attempted to pantomime the action but, each time, the children insisted that "he didn't look as if he were really driving." Suddenly Jack, who had been sitting on the sidelines, put up his hand and volunteered to try it. The vigorous and convincing pantomime he created, as he guided his cart around the stone, astonished the class. His position in the group changed at that moment, and while he never became one of the leaders, he was accepted, and often sought out. Working together in an atmosphere of give-and-take is an experience in democratic partnership; it provides the opportunity for the Jacks in the group to contribute their skills and have them accepted. Or, as a college student once put it, after her first experience of being in a play: "Now I know what John Glenn meant by 'we.' It was all of us working together who did it!"

An Opportunity to Build Social Awareness

Putting oneself in the shoes of another is a way of developing awareness and human understanding. By the time a player has decided who a character is, why he behaves as he does, how he relates to others and the way in which he handles his problems, he has come to know a great deal about him. Even the very young or inexperienced player may glimpse insights that help him in his understanding of people and, therefore, of living. Both literature and original stories provide the player with this opportunity to study human nature.

In one class of ten-year-olds, the teacher began the morning by asking the children to think of someone they had seen on their way to school who had attracted their attention. It was suggested that the person should have interested them enough to become a character in a play. Immediately, every hand went up and a variety of people were described. After a period of telling what they looked like, where they were, who they might have been, and what they were doing, the teacher asked the class to select three who would be good subjects for original stories. The class was then divided into three groups, of six or seven each, and given an opportunity to make up a story centered around the person of their choice.

The first group decided upon the character Peter suggested—an old man whom he described sitting on the steps of his apartment building. The children decided the old man might have been a school janitor, who, in his retirement, spent the morning watching the children go to school. Having reached this decision, it was no time at all until they had developed a plot in which the old man's memory of having once saved a child's life became a sudden reality: A boy had run across the street after his ball, and the old man, in an automatic reaction, had rescued him from being hit by a car. The story, with its throwback scene imposed on the present, was dramatic and exciting both to the players and to the rest of the class; more than that, however, was the warm and sympathetic portrayal of the old man. Two adults, who were in the room that day, have spoken many times of the scene. If the memory remained with the observers, is it not likely that the children, who created the play, must have grown in the process?

A Healthy Release of Emotion

Much has been said about the thinking, both creative and critical, that characterizes creative dramatics. There is another value, however, which is of equal importance and this is the opportunity to feel and release emotion. As children grow up, the opportunity for emotional response is too often restricted to television and movies. While there is value in being a spectator, the deep involvement of active participation is lacking.

Control of emotion does not mean suppression of emotion. It means the healthy release of strong feeling through appropriate and acceptable channels. At some time or another, all people feel anger, fear, anxiety, jealousy, resentment, and negativism. Through the playing of a part in which these emotions are expressed, the player may release them and thus relieve tension. "By permitting the child to play freely in a setting of security and acceptance, we enable him to deal satisfactorily and healthfully with his most urgent problems." [6]

Better Habits of Speech

To many teachers, one of the primary values of creative dramatics is the opportunity it offers for training in speech. There is a built-in motivation, for the player wishes to be heard and clearly understood. Volume, tempo and pitch, as well as diction, are involved in a natural way; no other form of speech exercise captures the player to the same degree or offers so good a reason for working on speech. The little girl who can barely be heard in a classroom recitation will be reminded by her fellow players to speak up or the lines will be lost. And the boy with the strident tone will also be told when his voice is too loud or inappropriate for the char-

---

6. Ruth Hartley, Lawrence K. Frank and Robert M. Goldenson, *op. cit.*, p. 16.

acter he is portraying. Being, in turn, a giant, a prince, a king, an an old man, or an animal, offers further opportunity for developing variation of tone and expression. In creative drama, the concern is less for a standard of speech than it is for audibility, clarity, and expression. While the teacher does not dwell on speech as the major objective, she can point out its importance, and the children will accept the validity of her suggestion.

Not only articulation but vocabulary is served through this form of oral expression. Conceptual thinking and the cognitive aspect of language are encouraged when words are put into practical use. For the young child, the culturally disadvantaged child, or the student with a foreign language background, vocabulary can be built, and distinctions in word meanings made clear through participation in creative dramatics. Even abstract learnings may come more readily when words are acted or shown.

An Experience with Good Literature

The story one plays makes a lasting impression. Therefore, the opportunity to become well acquainted with good literature, through dramatizing it, is a major value—not that every story chosen will be of high literary quality. But many will be, and the leader usually discovers that these are the stories that hold interest longest. Both folk tales and modern tales provide fine opportunities for acting; a program that includes a variety of material helps to build appreciation and set a standard for original writing. Television shows and comic books attract temporary interest; but put beside a story that has stood the test of time, these do not sustain attention. Believable characters, a well-constructed plot, and a worthwhile theme make for engrossing drama. What better way of discovering and learning to appreciate literature?

An Introduction to the Theatre Arts

While creative dramatics is primarily participant-centered, it deals with the basic materials of drama and thus offers the young player his first taste of the magic and make-believe of the theatre.

In his imagination, a chair becomes a throne; a stick, a wand; a change in lighting, a difference in time; and a character, a human being in whom he believes and with whom he can identify. Listening, watching, and becoming involved are required of the theatre audience. The child who is introduced to the theatre, first through playing, is going to look for more than superficial entertainment when he attends a performance.

SUMMARY

Creative dramatics, whether in the classroom or in the camp or community program, may be regarded as a way of learning, a means of self-expression or an art form. Children are helped to assume responsibility, accept group decisions, work together cooperatively, develop new interests, and—particularly in a classroom situation—seek new information. "It is at once the most completely personal, individualistic and intimate, as well as the most highly socialized art." [7]

The values of informal play are many, and the leader will discover these, and others, as the group moves and grows. Not all of the values listed will be manifested at once, or perhaps ever, for the creative process is slow and takes time to develop. It is often said that few people ever perform on their highest level. This is true of the beginning player, child or adult, who, through shyness or actual fear, needs encouragement and acceptance.

The sensitive leader recognizes this and tries to create an atmosphere of mutual trust. In his acceptance of every child and what he has to offer, the leader has taken the first big step toward building self-confidence. Freedom will follow, and an ordinary room will become a place in which exciting things can happen.

---

7. Harold Rugg and Ann Shumaker, *The Child-Centered School* (Cleveland: The World Book Company, 1928), p. 264.

CHAPTER 2

Imagination is the Beginning

Imagination and creativity are two words we hear a great deal about these days. Whether we are able to define them precisely, or whether we merely have a sense of their meanings, we use them freely, and in regard to a variety of people and a multitude of activities. The purist may object to the coining of such terms as "creative furniture," or "imaginative setting," yet our continued and widespread usage in regard to both people and products has made them household words.

The *fact* of imagination has long been recognized, but it is only recently that the *value* of imagination has been hailed. Shakespeare described imagination as the spark that makes man "paragon of animals." Today, not only the artist but business men, scientists, military leaders, and educators describe imagination as the magic force that goes beyond the mastery of facts and techniques in the search for new ideas. While it is not the purpose of this book to go into the subject in either length or depth, the terms imagination and creativity have been used in describing the art of creative drama. Therefore, some definition is required.

CREATIVITY

Creativity may be defined in a number of ways. It may be thought of in terms of product or process, depending on whether we are concerned with the solution to a problem, or the way in which the problem is solved. If creativity is interpreted as process, it is considered as a new way of seeing, a different point of view, an original idea, or a new relationship between ideas. Inventiveness and adaptation are often included in the thinking of those who believe creativity to be a way of working.

If, on the other hand, creativity is defined in terms of product, it is best illustrated by works of art (poems, stories, paintings, music, dance), scientific inventions, and new arrangements or designs. There has been great interest in the study and measurement of creativity in recent years, and a considerable body of data has appeared. One of the assumptions, accepted by psychologists doing research, is that creativity is not a special gift possessed by a fortunate few but, rather, a human capacity possessed to some degree by all men. It has been found, incidentally, that many individuals learn more if permitted to approach their studies creatively.

According to some authorities, the beginning of creative thinking may be found early in the life of the infant, in his "manipulative and exploratory activities." [1] In his awareness of human expression, gestures, and sound, the baby is first observer and then investigator. It is but a short step from here to his own experimentation, at which point he becomes creator. Drama, both informal and formal, is man's artistic creation, based on his observation of human life —selected, arranged, and heightened.

The words—observer, investigator, creator—are, therefore, of particular interest to the teacher of creative dramatics. One leader held a discussion on the subject of creativity and imagination with a group of eight-year-olds in a creative dramatics class. Their dialogue ran something like this:

Teacher: What does creativity mean to you?
Patricia: I think it means to make.
Denise: No, not to make. To make up.
Teacher: Can you explain the difference?
Kenny: Well, if a man made a pair of shoes, he'd be creating.
Teacher: Do you all agree with Kenny?
Denise: No, I think only the first pair of shoes would be created. If the man made a lot of others like them, they'd just be made—not made up.
Teacher: Then everything that's made is not created?

---

1. Paul E. Torrance, "Creativity," *What Research Says* Series (Washington: National Education Association of the United States, 1963).

Denise: (Sticking to her original point) Only the things that aren't copied.

Teacher: You don't get any fun out of copying.

Patricia: How do you feel about copying?

Cathy: I think it's all right to copy some things.

Teacher: What kind of things, Cathy?

Cathy: Well, like good manners. And words. You wouldn't know what to do lots of times if you didn't have something to copy.

Teacher: Then you don't think copying is always a bad thing to do?

(General agreement that it is not)

Denise: Just the same, you shouldn't use somebody else's mind. You want a thing to be just yours.

Alan: You have to know what to copy and what not to. Sometimes it's hard to know which is which.

Teacher: How would you explain imagination? Dean?

Dean: You think of something that isn't there.

Teacher: Would anyone else like to add to that?

Billy: Yes, it isn't that it isn't there. It's more like you make yourself believe.

Patricia: You see, outside of you it isn't real. Inside your head, it's there.

Teacher: Do you enjoy using your imagination?

John: Oh, yes. Because you can make anything happen.

Patricia: Sometimes they're silly things. What we do isn't always good.

Teacher: What do you mean, "not good"?

Patricia: I mean, some children have better ideas than others.

Teacher: But you still want a chance to try them all out?

Denise: Oh, yes. It's better for an idea to be yours than good.

Billy: I think using your imagination means being creative. It means making up something that wasn't ever there before.

The discussion went on like this for some time, but it was obvious that the terms, creativity and imagination, held real meaning for the children. Their observations—that it is important to have ideas and the freedom to try them out—are basic to good work in creative dramatics.

IMAGINATION: BEGINNING EXERCISES

The first day the class meets, the leader will do well to begin with the simplest of exercises in which imagination is involved. Regardless of age level, there must be an opportunity for the participants to go beyond the here and now, but they cannot, and should not, be expected to handle a story or create an improvisation. It is also wise to begin with the entire group, if space permits. This removes all thought of audience, thereby diminishing fear and self-consciousness.

How the leader begins will be determined by the age, experience, and number in the group, as well as the size of the playing space. If the group is fortunate in having a very large room, physical movement is an excellent opening exercise. Music or even a drumbeat will enhance the mood and help to focus the attention. One simple and very effective way of beginning is to have the group walk to the beat of the drum. As the group becomes more comfortable and relaxed, the beat can be changed: rapid, double time, slow, and so on. The participants, in listening for the change in beat, forget themselves and are usually able to use their entire bodies. Galloping, skipping, and hopping are fun for younger children, and good exercise for those much older. Adults find freedom and pleasure in physical movement and sit down when it is over—relaxed, and better able to go on to the next assignment.

From the purely physical body movement, the teacher may move on to mood. For example, if the group has been walking to a beat, he may suggest that there is green grass underfoot. "How does it feel to you? Your feet are tired. Think what it is like to put them down on soft, cool grass. Take off your shoes. (Some will do so at this suggestion.) Walk on it. Feel it."

Soon the steps will become more flexible as the image of grass grows stronger. The teacher might suggest, next, that there is ice underfoot. "It is hard, slippery, difficult to walk on, dangerous." The movement usually changes perceptibly now as the participants imagine the difficulties of crossing an icy pavement. Muscles are tensed and bodies stiffen. It is here that one or two may lose their balance or even slip and fall down as they get into the spirit of the situation. The teacher's acknowledgment of their efforts offers encouragement, and usually stimulates further invention. Imagining that they are running across hot sand, stepping over puddles, crossing a creek, wading through snow—each suggestion stretches the imagination a little more. When the exercise is over, most groups will have moved far from the first stiff, self-conscious steps without realizing when, or how, or even that they have done it.

Games, known to all the participants, might come next. Tossing a ball is a familiar activity, and the players, by this time, usually respond eagerly. The teacher may suggest that they are using a tennis ball, then a basketball, next a beach ball, or a Ping-Pong ball. The players experience little difficulty shifting from one ball to another, and have fun showing its size and weight as they throw and catch it. Lively groups sometimes drop the ball, run for it, lose it, or carry the assignment much farther then the leader suggested. Favorite activities such as flying kites, jumping rope, playing hopscotch, and playing with jacks provide other opportunities for using the imagination. How long this goes on is best left to the discretion of the teacher, who can tell when the interest begins to wane.

A pantomime of seasonal sports might be the culmination of the various exercises, and a means of tying them together. If the class is large, it may be the time to subdivide into smaller groups, with each taking a particular game or sport. However the teacher proceeds from here, he will find that imagination has been sparked and the next step will be easier.

CONCENTRATION

If imagination is the beginning, concentration—the capacity to hold an idea long enough to do something about it—must come next. It is not enough to glimpse an idea; the image must be held long enough for action to follow. Inexperienced players of any age may have difficulty here, for self-consciousness and fear of failure are paralyzing agents. It is now that the teacher needs to encourage every effort, however small, in order to free the player of his self-doubt. This is difficult in some cases: the player may never have excelled at anything and so does not believe that he has anything worthwhile to offer. Many children, on the other hand, become involved easily. Concentration poses no problems for them because of their freedom from fear and their willingness to experiment.

ORGANIZATION

Concentration and organization go hand in hand. Once the players are able to focus their attention on their material, they can get down to the business of organizing it. They have ceased to think about themselves, and are ready to decide such things as who their characters are, what they are doing, and the overall form the improvisation will take. If the group is working on a story, the organization will more or less follow the plot. The characters are related to a logical sequence of events and it is up to the players to decide how they will handle them.

If, on the other hand, the group is creating an original situation —pantomime or improvisation—a different kind of planning is involved. More guidance is required, since there is no structure to follow, but if children feel free to experiment, they come up with surprising and often delightful results. "Organization" does not mean the imposing of a conventional form, but, rather, an arrangement of parts or material, so as to achieve order. Older groups, or groups that have had more exposure to television, movies, and theatre, are less inclined to experiment with organization although, with encouragement, they can be helped to find the challenge in "trying it another way." Organization is order, and until it exists in some form or another, the participants rarely find satisfaction in creative playing.

SELF-EXPRESSION

So far, we have been talking about exercises that may or may not be expressive. Creative dramatics implies self-expression, hence the necessity of the participant's involvement beyond merely imitating an action. How does he feel when the kite soars high in the air? Who is winning the ball game? How do we know? How many jacks has he won? Does he enjoy picking flowers in the woods? What are his feelings as he fishes, or rows his boat against a strong current? These are the kinds of questions we may ask as the players grow more confident.

We are not concerned with the quality of the child's performance yet; rather, we are concerned with his developing freedom and the ability to express himself. Each child has something to say, something that he alone can offer, provided he is given the opportunity and the encouragement. No one has put this any better than Hughes Mearns:

> You have something to say. Something of your very own. Try to say it. Don't be ashamed of any real thought or feeling you may have. Don't undervalue it. Don't let the fear of what others may think of it prevent you from saying it. Perhaps not aloud but to yourself. You have something to say, something no one in the world has ever said in just your way of saying it—but the thing itself is not half so important to you as what the saying will be to you.[2]

COMMUNICATION

Although communication is the responsibility of the formal theatre, and therefore not our primary concern, there comes a time when the participants want to share their work in creative dramatics, and this sharing involves communication skills. It has been stated that, for the younger child, public performance is undesirable; for the older child, under the right conditions, it may do no harm. But unless the class is exceptionally small, there will be periods of time when some are observers and some are participants. It is to these periods that communication pertains. This is the audience that is not an audience in the usual sense. On the other hand, the observers want to see and hear, and they become

2. Hughes Mearns, *Creative Power* (New York: Dover Publications, Inc., 1958), p. 259.

deeply involved in the situation. The participant soon learns that he must move on to the next stage of development: that of making himself clear, of being heard and understood, and of being interesting—in short, of communicating.

Communication comes about quite naturally in the discussion periods that follow each playing. One procedure, used successfully by many teachers, is the playing, discussing, replaying method. Or, to describe it more fully, the teacher begins with the story, which she either reads or tells to the group. This is followed by class discussion, in which the characters are enumerated and described, the plot is reviewed, and the scenes are planned. No matter how simple the story, it is important that it be thoroughly understood before the first playing. The group will decide which characters are necessary to the plot, which ones may be eliminated, or whether others should be added. Often a story, which is excellent to read, takes considerable adapting to make it good drama.

When the teacher is sure that the group has all details well in mind, he is ready to suggest playing it. Asking for volunteers usually brings a show of hands from which the teacher will choose the first cast. The players come forward, while the rest of the class remain in their seats. After they have finished the scene, the teacher leads a general discussion. This evaluation period covers the plot and the way the children have handled it. The players themselves always have criticisms to offer, but the observers also have reactions to share. Children's criticism is honest and their observations are keen. Because the observers anticipate playing the story themselves, they are as deeply involved as the players. Such questions as these help to guide the discussion:

1. Did they tell the story?
2. Was anything important left out?
3. What did you like about the way they began it?
4. Did we understand the ending?
5. When we play it the next time, what might we add or leave out?

The questions are naturally more specific when we have a particular story in mind. There will be further discussion of characters, their relationships and motives, but these usually come after a second or third playing. Finally, when the teacher feels that a number of important points have been made and the class is growing eager to resume playing, a second group is given a chance to play the same scene. This group, having the benefit of observation and discussion, will probably succeed in developing more detail and clearer characterizations. This does not necessarily happen, for the first group to volunteer may have been the stronger.

At any rate, when the second cast has finished, a new evaluation period is in order. It is always interesting to hear the different kinds of comments which this second discussion evokes. A third playing, a fourth, even a fifth may follow, depending on the interest of the children and the length of the period. It is a good idea to take the cue from them as to when to move on to the next scene. As long as the scene holds their interest, they will continue to grow in their understanding of it. The teacher will become increasingly sensitive to their involvement as they work together.

As the group gains experience, its ability to communicate increases. Younger children, because of their more limited vocabulary, communicate more easily through body movement and facial expression. Older children are not only better able to express themselves verbally but enjoy improvising dialogue. The adult student, depending on his background and previous experience, will feel more comfortable in one medium or the other. If the teacher begins with movement and pantomime, however, he will find that dialogue flows easily once the player has overcome his self-consciousness.

PROBLEMS IN CREATIVE PLAYING

Sooner or later, the teacher of creative dramatics, or the classroom teacher who uses creative dramatics, is bound to encounter problems of one sort or another. They may be simple problems of time and space: periods that are too short; space that is inadequate; classes that are too large. These problems can be solved, though the solutions are not always easy. They call for adaptability and ingenuity on the part of the leader, and present difficulties that are discouraging and sometimes defeating. Other problems confronting the leader, even under the most ideal circumstances, are the individual problems he finds in the group. It has been stated many times that self-consciousness is the greatest obstacle to creative playing. Self-consciousness, or fear, takes many forms. The shy child and the show-off are the two most frequently encountered. The insensitive child is also a problem, for he usually lacks friends, and so finds it difficult to work cooperatively in a group. And, finally, there is the handicapped child whose physical, mental, or emotional problems pose special difficulties for the leader.

There is great interest in drama as therapy at the present time, but this is a special field for which the average teacher—even the specialist in creative dramatics techniques—is not trained. Every teacher is aware of the therapeutic value of the arts, even though the primary purposes are educational and aesthetic. But because there are, in every group, those children (or adults) who experience real difficulty in expressing themselves, consideration must be given to their problems. If the problem is severe, it should be handled by a therapist and not the classroom teacher; in many cases, an intelligent, sympathetic effort to build self-respect and bring fun into the lives of the players can go a long way toward solving the problems.

Timidity

The timid child is the most common problem the teacher encounters, but one that creative dramatics can help. Such a child is usually quiet in a class, preferring to sit in the back of the room and let others do the talking. His fear of making a mistake, or even of being noticed, causes him to withdraw, even though down underneath he is eager to express his ideas and take part. He is usually not a happy child, for his feeling of inadequacy inhibits both expression and communication.

The little girl who never volunteers will need special encouragement to try doing a part, no matter how simple. The teacher, who gives her this opportunity to show her peers what she can do, may be taking the first step in helping her build a better self-image. If she is successful, it will be less difficult for her a second time.

The teacher will be wise to praise her warmly for whatever contribution she makes. Remember that, for her, the very fact of getting up in front of the class is a big achievement.

There was eight-year-old Patty, who was referred to a Saturday morning play group because of her excessive shyness. At first she took part only when the whole group was moving, and then because it would have been more conspicuous to remain seated than to get up with the others. After several weeks (probably five or six sessions) she did a pantomime of a child finding a kitten. Her honest joy and tenderness as she fondled its soft body drew spontaneous admiration from the other boys and girls in the class. This was the break-through. From that day Patty's eagerness to play was apparent. Her voice was small—inaudible at first—but grew stronger in proportion to her growing self-confidence. This was no sudden miracle; in fact, it took three years for the transformation to take place. Patty's feeling of inadequacy had been so deep-seated that many successes were necessary to convince her that she had something to offer that her peers would accept. Today she is not only one of the most vocal children in the group—she is an unquestioned leader. Whether she would have found her way anyhow, no one can say. Creative dramatics as a technique was deliberately used, and the change during her three years in the class was striking.

Showing Off

The show-off is just as much in need of help as the shy child but he rarely elicits the same kind of sympathetic attention. His problem is also one of uneasiness, and in trying to prove his importance, he does all the wrong things. His behavior will range from monopolizing the class discussion to interfering with the work of the other children (pinching, pushing, interrupting). He may deliberately use a wrong word for the sake of a laugh. He is conscious of the effect he is having, and so has difficulty concentrating on what he is doing.

An example is John, a nervous little fellow of nine, with facial mannerisms and a habit of interrupting. John was accepted by the others: he amused them. For more than a semester John's work was erratic. He seemed unable to get involved in a part for more than a minute or two, and then he would look around the room to see what effect he was having on the rest of the class. There was no sudden or dramatic incident that effected a change; rather, it was a long period of working under the patient guidance of a teacher who took every opportunity to praise his honest expression and help him to find satisfaction in getting attention legitimately. By the end of a year, John was able to work cooperatively with the group much of the time, and forego showing off. His problem was still not entirely solved but he had learned something of the give-and-take of working together, and the pleasure of recognition that comes from work that is honest.

Sometimes the teacher may be forced to ask the disruptive child to go back to his seat. Not punishment, but the consequences of unacceptable behavior will teach him that creative dramatics demands consideration and teamwork.

Insensitivity

The insensitive player is similar to, but different from, the show-off, in that he is usually rejected by the others and does not understand why. His clowning brings no laughter and he has great difficulty in making friends. He tends to reject the ideas of others and criticizes their efforts, often harshly. Playing a variety of roles may cause him to gain insights and develop an awareness of the feelings of others. Patient attention to his problem in human relations may, in time, help him to listen, and learn to accept suggestions from his peers. His is a difficult problem, but once he has begun to feel some small acceptance, he will prefer belonging to going it alone. Again, we are not talking about the extreme personality disorder but about the human being who is experiencing difficulty in working cooperatively with others.

Physical Handicaps

Children with special handicaps need special attention. Their teachers need special orientation to their special needs. While the classroom teacher may have a child who is crippled or who has a speech defect, he is not going to be equipped to practice therapy, or given time for all the help these special cases merit. If, however, he has one or two children in a group who are handicapped, he will treat them essentially as he does the others. These children need sympathy, understanding, and encouragement. The teacher must know what can be expected of them, and then try to adapt the activities to their capabilities. Often such a child will be in therapy, and if the teacher can work with the therapist, he will be able to receive helpful suggestions as to his approach.

For example, Marcia, who has a cleft lip and is seeing the speech therapist regularly, will benefit from an opportunity to use speech in a legitimate and pleasurable way. The teacher will not have the time to give her all the attention she needs, but in treating her like the others, and encouraging her in her efforts, he will be contributing to her social growth and, in some measure, to her treatment.

It is a common phenomenon that the stutterer often speaks fluently when cast in a play. While there is no proof that acting ever cured a stutter, the child who tends to repeat, or whose anxiety causes him to stutter, often finds relief in speaking as someone else. Regular participation in either informal or formal dramatics may have a therapeutic effect in encouraging successful oral expression.

Problems in Disadvantaged Urban Areas

Since the advent of the Headstart Program, we have been hearing much about the culturally disadvantaged child, or the child in the disadvantaged urban area. This is not a new problem in our society but one which, for a variety of reasons, is currently attracting wide attention, with funds allocated for the establishment of educational and recreational programs. The arts, including dramatic play and creative dramatics, are emphasized in many of these programs. The values cited in Chapter One have tremendous implications for these children, who have been born into an environment lacking books, playing space, supervision, the arts—and, in many cases, language itself. According to one group of leaders at a conference on the subject of *Creative Dramatics in Special Education,* recently held in New York City, the problems of these children are manifold. For example, poverty may preclude treatment of a physical handicap; the handicap causes feelings of inadequacy, and this results in emotional disturbance.[3] Hence, we have a combination of problems requiring understanding and skill beyond the qualifications of the average well-prepared teacher.

The need for special training is recognized, and many universities and organizations are offering it. Because this is a subject of specialized interest and content, it is beyond the scope of this book; but for those teachers and recreation leaders who are interested in working in disadvantaged areas, let it be said that creative dramatics and theatre are approved and exciting techniques.

All people gain in self-respect when their ideas are accepted and put into effect. The child with a problem has a special need for acceptance, and the teacher tries to find the best way in which he can meet it. Creative dramatics provides an ideal opportunity to help the timid child overcome his inhibitions; provides the show-off with a better way of getting attention; guides the insensitive child to some awareness of the feelings of others; works with the handicapped to find his avenue of self-expression; and broadens the horizons of the disadvantaged. "How drama can be used today, how the play-acting impulse can be harnessed to help people grow, to develop greater sensitivity to themselves and to their fellow human beings, to become more spontaneous and outgoing, to discard old fears and insecurities, has attracted the interest of many who are working in the various fields of human relations." [4]

SUMMARY

To summarize, imagination is the spark that sets off the creative impulse. Concentration (the capacity to hold an idea long enough to do something about it) and organization (the design or arrange-

---

3. Conference on *Creative Dramatics in Special Education,* sponsored by Region 14, Children's Theatre Conference, at Mills College of Education in New York City, April 8, 1967.

4. Jack Simos, *Social Growth through Play Production* (New York: The Association Press, 1957), p. 16.

ment of the parts) are necessary to satisfying self-expression. Communication—the bridge to others—comes last, and is less the concern of creative drama than of the formal play.

In all creative work there are obstacles. These must be recognized and overcome. They may be problems of time and space, or the more difficult ones of human relations. The wise creative dramatics leader learns first to identify the problems and then to look for solutions. He will remember that he is neither therapist nor theatre director but teacher, guiding players, whatever their age, in the medium of informal drama. Gerald Way[5] has suggested the role of the teacher in these words:

> Schools do not exist to develop actors but to develop people, and one of the major factors in developing people is that of preserving and enriching to its fullest the human capacity to give full and undivided attention to any matter in hand at any given moment.

---

5. Gerald Way, *Development through Drama* (London: Longmans, Green & Co., 1967), p. 15.

CHAPTER 3

Pantomime: The First Step

Pantomime is the art of conveying ideas without words. Children enjoy pantomime, and for the young child this is an excellent way to begin creative dramatics. Since many of his thoughts are spoken entirely through the body, the five-or six-year-old finds pantomime a natural means of expression. Group pantomimes of the simplest sort challenge the imagination and sharpen awareness. In kindergarten, such basic movements as walking, running, skipping, and galloping prepare for the creative use of rhythms. Music can set the mood for people marching in a parade, horses galloping on the plains, toads hopping in a field, or children skipping on a fine autumn day. In other words, rhythmic movement becomes dramatic when the participant makes use of it to become someone or something other than himself.

For older children and adults, pantomime is advocated because it encourages the use of the entire body and relieves the players of having to think of dialogue. Here, also, group pantomime should precede individual work. Familiar activities such as playing ball, flying kites, running for a bus, or hunting for a lost object get the group on its feet and moving freely. If the entire class works at one time, self-consciousness disappears and involvement is hastened. Fifteen or twenty minutes of this sort of activity, changed frequently enough to hold the group's interest, makes for relaxation, and readiness to move on to a more challenging assignment.

CLASS SIZE

While creative rhythms can be carried on successfully with any number, pantomime requires a group of no more than fifteen to twenty. If a class is very large, the teacher should make every effort to divide it so that half the group is involved with some other activity at that hour. Pantomime demands individual attention, and every child should be assured the opportunity of participation each time the class meets. This is true whatever the age level, for growth depends upon repeated experiences in exercises that increase in difficulty.

LENGTH OF CLASS PERIOD

The length and frequency of class meetings depend upon the situation (school, club, or camp) and the age of the players. With very young children, daily experiences for ten to fifteen minutes are ideal, whereas for older children, two or three meetings a week for forty-five minutes or an hour work out well. With club groups, the meeting may be only once a week; this is less desirable but may be all the time possible. High school students and young adults can be absorbed for as long as two hours, but, in general, more frequent meetings of shorter length are preferable.

In schools where creative dramatics is a definite part of the curriculum, the teacher can look forward to regular meetings throughout the year. Where it is not, it will be up to the classroom teacher to introduce it whenever and however she can. She will probably use pantomime in connection with other subjects which, if imaginatively done, can be of value as a tool for teaching and a creative experience for the class.

PLAYING SPACE

Whereas a stage is generally used in formal rehearsals, a large room is far more desirable for creative dramatics. Little children enjoy moving all over the room and should be encouraged to do so. The younger the group, therefore, the larger the space required. If a very large room is not available, a classroom in which all the chairs have been pushed aside will do. Space makes for freedom; a small or cramped area inhibits it. An auditorium with a stage and chairs is least desirable as a playing space for a beginning group of any age, since it inevitably leads to a concept of performance with stage techniques before the players are ready for it.

IMAGINATION

Whatever the space, however, the teacher will try to see that it is kept uncluttered and that the players are seated in a circle or semicircle around it. Having engaged in rhythms and group activities, the players are now ready for pantomime. There are many ways of proceeding, but one that has proved effective is having the class handle a small, nondescript object (such as a small box or eraser) as if it were several different items. For example, the teacher calls six or seven players to the center, hands one the object and tells him it is a diamond bracelet, the most beautiful piece of jewelry any of them has ever seen. He will then ask the players to:

1. Handle it.
2. Look at it.
3. React to it.
4. Pass it along to the next person.

When each has had a chance to handle and react to it, the teacher will say that it is now a kitten with very soft fur. The same group again takes it and reacts to it. The next time, it may be a wallet—dirty and torn—with nothing in it. The fourth time it is passed, it becomes a knife, or a glass of water filled to the brim, or perhaps an old and valuable manuscript. Each time it is handed around, the group invests it with more of the qualities of the suggested object. The idea, of course, is to stimulate the imagination and help the players realize that it is not the property used but their own imaginations that turn an eraser first into a bracelet, then a kitten, then a wallet, and finally a knife, or a glass of water.

The observers are as interested as the players in the growing reality that develops. Depending upon the time at their disposal, the teacher may repeat the exercise with another group, or move on to a new exercise. Some of the questions that might be asked of the observers are:

1. How did we know it was a bracelet?
   "One player held it so that the diamonds sparkled in the light." "John held it as if it were very expensive." "Linda tried it on." "Charles looked for the price tag."
2. Why did we know it was a kitten the second time the eraser was passed?
   "One stroked its head." "Another girl put it close to her cheek as if it were alive." "Barbara held its legs carefully when she gave it to Lois." "They all held it as if it were soft and round."

Questions put to the players might be:

1. What did the wallet look like to you?
   "It was dark green leather." "It was old and torn." "There was a faded snapshot in the front." "It had a hole in the bottom." "It was muddy because it had been lost in the yard."
2. You were careful not to let any of the objects drop, but you handled them differently. Why?
   "The bracelet was valuable." "I didn't want it to get broken." "The kitten was alive, and that made it different from all the others." "When I jiggled the glass, the water almost spilled."

Questions like these push the players to stronger visual images and greater power of observation.

Another exercise that serves to excite the imagination is the suggestion that a table in the middle of the room is covered with a variety of small objects. Each participant must go up and pick out one thing, showing by the way he handles it, what it is. While this is an individual exercise, it can be done with several persons at once so that the attention is not focused on a single player. By having the rest of the class seated in a semicircle, some observers will see one player and some another. This is fun for all, and what self-consciousness may have existed in the beginning will soon be gone.

CONCENTRATION

Many children will be able to concentrate on the exercises but some, for whom this is the first experience of this sort, will not, so the next step is to work on "holding the image." One good exercise is to have the class hunt for a ring that has been lost. A few minutes of searching usually involves them in the assignment. If it does not, the teacher might actually hide a ring and ask them to find it. The reality that comes with the second playing demonstrates clearly the difference between pretending to hunt and really looking. Other good group exercises for developing concentration are:

1. Watching a plane come in.
2. Looking at a funny movie.
3. Smelling smoke in the woods.
4. Listening for the lunch bell to ring.

SENSE IMAGES

The class is now ready for some specific exercises involving the five senses. This might be introduced by a discussion of the ways in which we find out what is going on around us. We see; we hear; we touch; we smell; we taste. Individuals may do the following, using no props, but trying to "see" what is suggested.

1. Enter a very large room in which you have left your sweater.
2. Go into a dark closet to look for your sweater.
3. Go into your own room to get your sweater.
4. Try to find your sweater among a dozen in the locker room.

Exercises for the sense of hearing might include:

1. Hearing an explosion.
2. Listening to a small sound and trying to decide what it is.
3. Listening to a military band coming down the street.
4. Hearing a dance orchestra playing a popular tune on the radio.

Exercises for the sense of smell might include:

1. Coming home from school and smelling cookies baking in the kitchen.
2. Walking in the woods and smelling a campfire.
3. Smelling different perfumes on a counter.
4. Smelling something very unpleasant and trying to decide what it is.

Exercises for the sense of taste might include:

1. Eating a piece of delicious chocolate candy.
2. Trying a foreign food that you have never tasted before, and deciding you like it.
3. Biting into a sour apple.

Exercises for the sense of touch might include:

1. Touching a piece of velvet.
2. Touching a hot stove.
3. Touching or holding an ice cube.
4. Touching or holding some sharp nails.

These are only a few suggestions, and the leader will think of many more. Whatever is suggested, however, should always be within the experience of the players. Practice in actual hearing and observation is good exercise and may be introduced either beforehand or at any point that the teacher thinks it of value. For instance, the teacher might ask the players to:

1. Close your eyes for one minute and listen to all the sounds you can hear.
2. Go to one corner of the room and describe all the things that you see.
3. Touch one object and describe it as completely as possible.

What we are trying to do is to "lead children into experiences that will involve them in touching, seeing, tasting, hearing, and smelling the things in their world. We also want them to become involved in experiences that will lead to imagining, exploring, reasoning, inventing, experimenting, investigating, and selecting, so that these experiences will not only be rich in themselves but lead to personal creative growth." [1]

---

1. Earl Linderman and Donald W. Herberholz, *Developing Artistic and Perceptual Awareness* (Dubuque: William C. Brown and Co., 1964), Introduction, p. x.

PERFORMING AN ACTION

There is no right or wrong order and no prescribed length of time the group should spend on one kind of exercise. Generally speaking, the older the players, the longer the attention will be sustained, but this does not always hold true. At any rate, a pantomime that is guaranteed to capture the interest of every player, regardless of age, is "making or doing something." In the beginning, the teacher will offer suggestions, but later, the players will have ideas of their own. Some good suggestions might be:

1. Setting a table.
2. Baking a cake.
3. Feeding your dog.
4. Getting dressed.
5. Doing your homework.

Again, let it be stressed that particularly in working with disadvantaged children, or children in urban areas, the activities suggested should be those in their environments. "Washing clothes" rather than "fishing in a brook" is familiar to these children, and can, therefore, be easily imagined and acted. This, incidentally, also helps children to respect their own ideas and regard their own experiences more positively.

Pantomimes of actions will grow more complicated as the players put them into situations. The above might be inherent in such scenes as the following:

1. You are getting ready for a birthday party for your sister, and must set the table. What are you going to put on it? Are there decorations? A cake? Favors? Presents? What dishes and silver will you use? Is it a surprise? Are you alone?
2. You are baking your first cake. No one is home, so you must read and follow the recipe yourself. What will you put in it? What utensils do you need? Is it a success?
3. You have a new puppy and have come home from school to take care of it. What do you feed it? How much? How big is he? What kind of dog?

4. You are getting up on a Saturday morning. Today it has begun snowing so you must dress to go out and play. What do you wear? Is it cold? Are you excited about it? Do you take time to comb your hair? Eat your breakfast?
5. It is after dinner and you have been told to do your homework. There is a television show you would like to see, but you know you should study. What is the assignment? Do you like the subject? Is it hard? Easy? Boring? What is the show you want to see? Is anyone else in the room? What do you finally do about it?

MOOD AND FEELINGS

Somewhere along the way, feelings have crept into the pantomimes so that a specific assignment on mood will now be appropriate. The teacher may want the group to talk about feelings first, or perhaps this will come about as a result of a particularly good job one of the players has done. The teacher might even ask the class what kinds of feelings they have experienced, and their responses will often include many more than he has anticipated. Anger, fear, happiness, excitement, pride, curiosity, vanity, anticipation, sorrow, and hatred are some that seven-and eight-year-olds have enumerated.

This might be a time to break the class into groups of four or five, with each group taking one feeling to pantomime. Delightful results are always forthcoming, when working on mood. One group showed excitement through a scene on Christmas Eve, when they crept downstairs to look at the tree and presents. Another asked if they could act out the story of *Pandora's Box* because it was such a good example of curiosity. Another group chose fear and set their scene in a tent at a summer camp. They were campers, who heard a strange noise at night and imagined it to be a bear, but it was only their counselor coming back.

It soon becomes obvious that more than one emotion is usually involved in a situation of any length. Therefore, the next step will be to show change of mood. Situations like the following help the players to move from one mood to another.

1. You are a group of friends taking a hike in the woods. It is a beautiful day and you find strawberries and wild flowers. You

stop to have your lunch, but when you are ready to move on, you discover that you have wandered from the path and are lost. Your happy mood changes to panic. Where are you? Should you go on, or turn back? Is there any familiar landmark to guide you? Suddenly one of the girls finds a broken flower lying on the ground. As she picks it up, she realizes that it is on the path, and she must have dropped it when she looked for a picnic spot. Panic turns to relief as the group starts for home.

2. A group of boys discover a cave (or it could be the basement of an empty building). They go in, curious as to what they may find. One of them stumbles over a box. The boys open it and find money and jewels. Excitement grows as they realize they have found hidden treasure. Then they hear voices; men are approaching. Terrified, the boys hide. The men go past, not seeing them. The boys stuff a few coins in their pockets and run, escaping from danger.
3. A group of people get into an elevator in a big downtown building. Suddenly it stops between floors. Their poise turns to fear as the operator pushes one button, then another, and nothing happens. Suddenly, she gets it started and the elevator moves, taking the passengers down to the ground level.
4. You are a group of children who come into your schoolroom one morning and find a monkey scampering about. First you are startled, then amused by his antics. Finally, the man who has lost him comes in and catches him, taking him away. You are sorry to see him go as he waves goodbye to you from his owner's shoulder.
5. You are going on a field trip to which you have looked forward for a long time. You get in the bus, but the bus will not start. After a few minutes, the driver lets you know that he cannot make it go, and so your trip must be postponed. Disappointed, you get out. Suddenly the engine starts. You turn around and see the driver motioning for you to get back in. Your happiness is great because you can now go after all.
6. You are sitting in a movie. First you are watching a very dull short. How do you feel when it seems to be going on forever? Then it changes to a hilariously funny cartoon. How do you react? At last, the feature begins and you are absorbed.

CHARACTERIZATION

Until now, we have been pantomiming activities, and working to induce mood or feeling. The next step is characterization. Some participants will already have suggested characters different from themselves but the teacher can use either the same exercises or new ones to start the group thinking in terms of characterization.

Again, situations involving groups is a good way to begin.

1. You are a group of people waiting for a bus on a city street. Each one of you will think of someone special to be: an elderly woman going to see her grandchildren, a business man late for work, a girl on her way to high school, a blind man who needs help getting on the right bus, a young man beginning a new job, etc.
2. You are pilgrims who have gone to a shrine where, once a year, one wish is said to be granted. Decide who you are and what it is you want. You might be a crippled man who wants to walk again, a poet who wants very much to have his work published, a young mother who wants her sick baby to be cured. The teacher may wish to play with the group and be the statue at the shrine who indicates which wish is to be granted. This is a good situation because it offers an opportunity to work on both characterization and strong motivation.
3. You are people in a bus terminal. Some of you are going on trips, others returning; still others are meeting friends or relatives. There may be a porter, a man selling tickets, a man selling newspapers and magazines, etc. By your behavior, let us know who you are and how you feel as you wait for the buses to arrive and depart.

Some individual pantomimes stressing character are suggested:

1. You are a robber who is entering a house at night. While you are there, the people return unexpectedly. You listen and finally make your escape, having stolen nothing.
2. You are the neighborhood gossip. You have a party line, and one of your favorite pastimes is listening in on other people's

conversations. This afternoon you hear some very good news, some bad news, and then some remarks about yourself and your habit of listening in on your neighbors. How do you react? What do you do?

3. You are a child who has wanted a dog for a long time. One day you overhear your parents talking about it in the next room. Your mother does not want a dog, but your father thinks it is time you had one. They discuss reasons for and against it. How do you react to their arguments and what is the final decision?
4. Two of you will be a customer and a storekeeper in a shop in a foreign country. You do not know each other's languages. The customer decides, in advance, on three things he needs to buy and tries to convey what they are to the clerk, through pantomime. Who are you? What are the three things? How does it turn out? (This is an exercise which the entire class can do in pairs.)

Another exercise is to take one action and do it as three different people. For example:

1. You go into a restaurant to order a meal.
   Do it as:
   (a) A teen-age boy who is very hungry.
   (b) A middle-aged woman, who has very little appetite and sees nothing on the menu that she wants.
   (c) A very poor old man who is hungry but must limit his choice to what he can afford. What does each order? How does he eat it?
2. You are trying on dresses in a shop.
   Do it as:
   (a) A very fat woman who has trouble being fitted.
   (b) A young girl, looking for a pretty dress to wear to a dance.
   (c) A secretary who is trying to find the most appropriate dress to wear on her first day at work in a new job.
3. You are visiting an art museum. First you look at the exhibition as:
   (a) An artist who knows the painter whose work is on display.
   (b) A woman who thinks she should go to museums but does not appreciate the pictures.

(c) An elderly woman who has been ill and is enjoying visiting her favorite museum for the first time in many months.

4. You are exercising in a gymnasium. Do the exercises first as:
   (a) A young man who loves all athletics.
   (b) A fat man whose doctor has advised him to exercise to lose weight.
   (c) A child who has never seen gymnasium equipment before.

(What does each do and how does he feel about it?)

PANTOMIME SUGGESTED BY OTHER MEANS

There are some exercises that are fun to do and stimulate inventiveness but have nothing to do with familiar actions, mood, or characters. These are good as a change, and may be introduced any time the leader feels the group needs a new type of stimulation. Some ideas are:

1. Play music and ask the group to move in any way it suggests.
2. Ask each person in the class to represent a mechanical appliance. He does not operate it; he *becomes* it. Some very imaginative results may be expected such as: a pencil sharpener, an egg beater, a lawn mower, a hair drier, a record player, etc. This is a challenging exercise, guaranteed to break down all inhibitions.
3. Give each person a color and ask that he suggest it by means of movement, attitude, or characterization. This, incidentally, may be followed up with an improvisation in which the color becomes a person. For example: Mrs. White, Mrs. Black, Mrs. Blue, Mrs. Green, Mrs. Red, and Mrs. Yellow might be ladies at a tea. What are they like? How do they talk? How can we distinguish one from another?
4. Each person selects a property, and acts according to what it suggests to him. The following are usually good for stimulating imaginative reactions: a gnarled stick, a ruler, a gold bracelet, a broken dish, a sponge. Again the players do not use the properties; they become characters suggested by their qualities.
5. Be puppets. Try to imagine what it feels like to be controlled by strings. Imagine that you are being controlled, then dropped by the puppeteer. While there is an element of characterization involved, it is the feeling of the inanimate object being manipulated that interests us.

As the group progresses, organization improves and situations often develop into simple plots. The players are learning to use their entire bodies to express ideas, and are ready to add dialogue. Although improvisation, or informal dialogue, is the subject of the next chapter, the teacher will want to alternate exercises in pantomime and improvisation. No matter how advanced the group, pantomime is always good to work on from time to time because of the type of practice it offers.

Many teachers of children find that acting a story while it is read aloud is a good transition from pantomime to dramatization. Many stories can be done in this way, though some lend themselves to it better than others. One story, which has met with success with more than one group, is included here as an illustration. It is *The Little Scarecrow Boy*.[2]

THE LITTLE SCARECROW BOY

Margaret Wise Brown

Once upon a time, in a cornfield, there lived a scarecrow (he enters and takes his place), and his scarecrow wife (she enters and takes her place beside him), and their little scarecrow boy (he enters and joins his mother and father).

Every day of the world old man scarecrow would go out into the cornfield to make faces at the crows. (He crosses the room and takes up his position in the cornfield.) And every day of the world little scarecrow boy would want to come, too. (He goes to his father and pulls at his coat.) And every day of the world, old man scarecrow would say:

"No!
No, little boy,
You can't go.
You're not fierce enough to scare a crow.
Wait until you grow."

(He shows how high little scarecrow boy will have to grow. The little boy is discouraged and returns to his mother.)

---

2. Margaret Wise Brown, *Fun and Frolic* (New York: D. C. Heath and Co., 1955).

So, little scarecrow boy would have to stay home all day and just grow. (His mother holds up her hand to the height he will have to grow. First he stretches his neck, then he stands on his toes and finally he jumps but he does not reach her hand.) Every morning when the sun came up, (the sun crosses the room, smiling happily) old man scarecrow went out to the cornfield. He waved his arms and made terrible faces. Every day the crows cried, "Caw! Caw! Caw!" (The crows fly in and circle around the corn, then one by one each crow sees old man scarecrow, screams, and flies away.) He made such terrible faces that the crows would fly far, far away.

Every night, when the sun went down (The sun walks back across the playing space, smiling happily) old man scarecrow would go home (He goes to the mother and the little boy), and there he would teach little scarecrow boy how to make fierce faces. (He makes a face and the little boy imitates it.) One—two—three—four—five—six. Old lady scarecrow would clap her hands and whistle through her teeth at the looks of them.

One day after the little boy knew all six of his father's terrible faces so that he could make them one after the other, he decided to go out into the cornfield by himself and frighten a crow. (The scarecrows have closed their eyes in sleep.) So the next morning, before the sun was up, or old man scarecrow was up, or old lady scarecrow was up, little scarecrow boy got out of bed. (He steps forward cautiously.) He dressed and went quietly . . . (He takes one step.) . . . quietly . . . quietly . . . quietly out of the house and over to the cornfield. He stood in his father's place. (He takes his father's position in the cornfield.)

It was a fine morning and the sun came up. (The sun crosses the stage, smiling.) Far away over the trees, crows flew around and around. Little scarecrow boy waved his arms through the air. He had never felt fiercer in all his life. (The little boy waves his arms and makes faces.) In the distance the "caws" of the crows were heard. (The leader enters and all of the crows fly in, circling the corn. One crow at a time sees the little boy, screams and flies off. Only the leader is left and he is not afraid. He starts toward the little scarecrow boy.)

"Oh!" said little scarecrow boy, and he made his first fierce face. Still came flying the big crow.

"Oh, Oh!" said little scarecrow boy and he made his second fierce face. Still came flying the big crow. He made his third fierce face.

"Oh, oh, oh!" It was time to go. (He jumps down and runs in a circle, covering very little ground but running hard. The crow flies after him.)

So, little scarecrow boy ran and ran. Then he stopped. He made his fourth fierce face. Still came flying the big old crow. He ran and he ran and he made his fifth fierce face. Still came flying the big old crow. Little scarecrow boy had only one face left now. So he stopped. He held his arms wide above his head and he made his sixth fierce face. (As he makes his sixth face, the old crow stops, backs up, then turns and flies off.)

Whoa! The old crow stopped and then backwards flew through the air, feathers flying everywhere, until there wasn't even the shadow of a crow in the cornfield. A scarecrow at last!

(Meanwhile, old man scarecrow walks to his side.) Then little scarecrow boy saw a shadow in front of him and he looked around. There beside him stood his father. Old man scarecrow was proud of his little boy and shook his scarecrow hand. (They shake hands.) Old lady scarecrow was proud of her little boy, who could make all six fierce faces. (She pats him fondly.) And when little scarecrow boy grew up, he was the fiercest scarecrow in all the cornfields in all the world.

This is a somewhat shortened version of the story, with action suggested by one group of children. All took turns playing the different parts, and had a grand time creating fierce faces. One child read the story while the others acted it in pantomime. The scarecrows offered an opportunity to experiment with physical movement in addition to simple characterizations. Stories read, while acted, help the more timid or inexperienced children to follow the plot and feel the sense of accomplishment that comes from successful dramatization.

SUMMARY

Pantomime, while good practice at any time, is usually the most satisfactory way of beginning work in creative dramatics. Although it is not necessary to follow a prescribed program of exercises, it is easier for many groups to begin with familiar activities and then move on to mood, or feeling, and finally characterization. By starting with pantomime, the players learn to express themselves through bodily action, without the additional problem of dialogue. Younger children accept this as a natural means of expression, and older children and adults find it easier to begin with pantomime than with improvisation or formal acting. Pantomime sharpens perception and stimulates the imagination as players try to remember how actions are done and what objects are really like, as to size, weight, and shape. Recalling emotion demands concentration and involvement: How do you feel when you are happy, tired, angry, excited, anxious, etc.? Close observation of people is a means of developing believable characters whose bearing, movement, and gestures belong to them and whose behavior seems appropriate. Although pantomime is considered here as a medium of expression, it may become an art form in itself: mimes like Marcel Marceau have demonstrated its power to communicate with people of all ages and backgrounds, when a high level of artistry is achieved.

CHAPTER 4

Improvisation: Characters Speak

Improvisation is difficult at first. Dialogue does not flow easily, even when it has been preceded by much work in pantomime and a thorough understanding of the situation or story. With practice, however, words do begin to come, and the players discover the possibilities of character development when oral language is added. Dialogue is apt to be brief and scanty at first but usually begins to flow rapidly, once the children become accustomed to it. Players, aged seven and older, enjoy the opportunity of using words to further a story and more fully describe the characters they are portraying. It is a good idea to begin with simple situations so as to get used to using dialogue before attempting more ambitious material.

Many of the situations suggested in the previous chapter on pantomime can be used, although they were designed with movement in mind. Frequently, children will begin to add dialogue of their own free will, as they feel the need of expressing ideas in words. When this happens, the leader accepts it as a natural progression from one step to the next. Younger children, players for whom English is a second language, or older students who lack self-confidence, will usually wait until they are urged to try adding dialogue. The teacher will not expect too much and will accept whatever is offered, knowing that more will be forthcoming the next time. The author recalls a sixth-grade class that was acting *The Story of Roland.* Although fond of the story and well oriented to the background, the first time it was played, one scene went like this: "Hello, Roland."—"Will you marry me?"—"Why, Roland, I'd love it." The final playing, after several had tried and discussed it, was a charming scene with all the necessary exposition and appropriate vocabulary.

Since even the simplest stories present complications for the beginner, some preliminary exercises are suggested. The purpose here is to give emphasis to dialogue rather than to the memorization or plot. Sometimes just one scene of a story can be improvised to advantage. The teacher will feel his way, and if the interest is sustained better with excerpts from favorite stories, he may prefer them to exercises.

Sounds, incidentally, can stimulate imagination and lead the listener to the creation of an improvisation. For example, the teacher can beat a drum or tambourine, knock, ring bells, or make any other kind of sound. This works particularly well with younger children but is a good exercise to use from time to time with those who are older.

SIMPLE IMPROVISATIONS BASED ON SITUATIONS

The following improvisations may be done on various age levels, although the backgrounds of the players will determine the appropriateness. In some cases, the situations are better for older players.

1. You are a group of people in a subway station. It is six o'clock in the evening. In the center is a newsstand, at which newspapers, magazines, and candy are sold. It is run by a woman who has been there for many years. She knows the passengers who ride regularly, and is interested in them and all the details of their daily lives. Decide on who you are going to be—a secretary, an actress, a businessman, a cleaning woman, a shopper, a policeman, a teen-ager, a stranger in town, etc. Then let us know all about you through your conversation with the proprietor of the newsstand, while you are waiting for your train.
2. The scene is a toyshop on Christmas Eve. It is midnight, and the owner has just closed the door and gone home. At the stroke of twelve the toys come alive and talk together. They may consist of a toy soldier, a rag doll, a beautiful doll, a clown, a teddy bear, a jack-in-the-box, etc. Let us know by your conversation and movements who you are and why you were not sold.
3. You are a committee from your school, assigned the job of

selecting a gift for your teacher, who is retiring. Each of you has an idea of what you think is appropriate, and you have only a certain amount of money to spend. The scene takes place in a large gift shop. Let us know who you are and what you want to buy. What is the decision you finally make?

4. This improvisation is good on a high school or college level. The scene is a meeting of the student council. You have the job of questioning a student who is reported to have stolen the examination questions for a history class. She is brought before you, and you ask her questions. What is each one of you like? How do you handle the situation? Is she guilty or not? What is your final decision and what do you do about it?
5. This improvisation is also probably better for older students, although it has been done by ten- and eleven-year-olds. You are a group of people returning for your thirty-fifth reunion from high school or college. Who are you? What has happened to you since you last saw each other? Have you been happy, successful, or unsuccessful? Let us know all about you through your conversation.
6. You are a group of young women in a suburban community. One of you has invited the new neighbor in to meet the rest of the group. Coffee is served and you talk together. All seems to be going well when the hostess notices that an expensive silver tray is missing from her coffee table. One by one, you begin to suspect the newcomer. Why do you suspect her? Did she take it? Is it found? Where? If she took it, why did she? Let us know what each one of you is like by your reaction to this situation. How does it turn out?
7. This improvisation is good with children. You are a group of children in an apartment house. It is Valentine's Day, and you are gathered in the front hall to look at and count your valentines. You see one child in the building going to her mailbox, and you notice that she did not receive any. How do you feel about this? What is each one of you like? Do you decide to do anything about it? If so, what do you do?
8. You are a group of children who live near a very cross, elderly woman. She chases you away from her property whenever you come near it. This particular morning, you see that someone has broken her fence and ruined many of her flowers. For the first time you feel sorry for her. What do you do? How does she

react to you? Do you all agree as to whether you should help her? Do your actions change her attitude toward children?

9. A new child has entered your class at school. He does not speak much English, and some of the children laugh at him. When recess comes, you all go out to the playground. How does each of you treat him? How does he react to you? You are all different so you will each feel differently toward him. Do you finally take him in, or do you exclude him? Try changing roles so that different players have the experience of trying the part of the new child. Does the improvisation change as you all think more about the situation?
10. The scene is a small bakery. One of you is the owner, one of you a child who helps him on Saturdays, and another is a beggar. It is not busy this particular morning so the owner goes out for coffee. While he is gone, a beggar comes into the shop and asks for some bread. The girl (or boy) knows that she should not give away the bread but she feels sorry for the old man. What do they say to each other? What does the owner say when he comes back? Try changing parts in this improvisation to see if it will turn out differently.

IMPROVISATIONS SUGGESTED BY OBJECTS

Not only situations and stories motivate improvisation; some very imaginative results can be obtained by the use of objects or properties. Try some of the following suggestions as springboards.

1. An object (any object) is put in the center of the circle where all the players can see it. Look at it, without speaking, for three or four minutes. Try to think of a story about it. Where might it have come from? How did it get here? What does it make *you* think of? Each of you will have an original story to tell; tell it.
2. This time, divide the class into groups of three or four. An object is presented, and each group is asked to make up an improvisation about it. Perhaps the property is a wooden spoon. When used with one class, the following ideas were suggested and these situations improvised.

   (a) The scene was a settler's cabin over one hundred years ago.

The family had very few household items and so they prized each one. Among them was a wooden spoon. In this scene it was used to stir batter for cornbread, and then washed and put carefully away.

(b) The scene was a museum, and the spoon a relic from the Indians who once inhabited the region. The characters were the curator of the museum and two children who were visiting it. The curator answered their questions by telling the history of the spoon.

(c) The scene was a cave. Three boys were hiking and found the spoon. They used it to dig, and discovered an old box of coins that had been buried there. They took the old spoon home with them for good luck.

(d) The scene was an industrial arts class. The boys were making things of wood, and a blind boy carved the spoon. It was so well done that the teacher said he would display it as one of the best things made in his class that year.

(e) The scene was a dump. The old wooden spoon was the speaker as he told the other pieces of trash how he had been used and handed down from one generation to the next. Finally his family became rich and threw him away because they considered him too old and ugly to be of further use to them.

Any object can function as a springboard, and no two groups will see it in exactly the same way. Among the kinds of properties that suggest ideas are:

A velvet jewelry box
An artificial rose
A foreign coin
A feather duster
A bell
An old hat
A cane
A quill pen
An old dog leash

An improvisation with unusual interest was developed from a whistle by a very imaginative group of ten-year-olds. They decided that it was a policeman's whistle, made of silver and bearing an inscription. They laid the scene in his home on the day of his retirement from the force; the characters were the policeman, his wife, and his grandson. The policeman came in that evening, took off his whistle, looked at it nostalgically a long time, then laid it on the supper table. His grandson, coming into the room at that point, begged him to tell the story again of how he had received it. As the story began, there was a throwback scene, in which the policeman was rescuing a child from burning in a bonfire many years before. He was honored for his bravery and given an inscribed silver whistle, which he treasured for the rest of his life. At the finish of the story, the throwback scene faded and some neighbors came in with a cake and presents for him. The improvisation was effective both in its good dramatic structure and the reality of the characterizations.

Not every group is able to develop an improvisation to this degree, but occasionally one will, and when it happens, it is an inspiration to the rest of the class. Incidentally, it is nearly always the result of the play's having been based on familiar material so that the players are sure of the dialogue and can identify easily with the characters. Again, respect for their background, and acceptance of the ideas that come out of it, not only make for comfort but bring forth ideas that the teacher probably would not have thought of. Children of foreign background have a wealth of material on which to draw, but too often it remains an untapped source because they have been made to feel that it is unworthy of consideration. Both the stories they have been told and the details of their everyday life contain the basic ingredients of drama. For example, one group of boys, who lived in a housing project, played a scene in an elevator. The situation was simple but had reality. Two boys, having nothing to do, decided to ride up and down in the elevator, angering the tenants and almost causing a tragedy because one man on a high floor was ill and waiting for the doctor. Whether or not this had been an actual experience the teacher did not know, but the situation contained reality, humor, and drama, with characters who were believable.

One final example of the use of properties was an improvisation done by a group of high school girls. They had been asked by the teacher to empty their purses and select the six most unusual or interesting objects. The objects they finally chose were a newspaper clipping, a snapshot, a lipstick in a Japanese case, a key ring with a red charm, a pocket knife, and a purse flashlight. Within minutes they had created a mystery, prompted by and making use of every one of the properties they selected. There were six players, and their preparation time was approximately ten minutes.

IMPROVISATIONS FROM COSTUMES

Similar to the use of props, and equally effective in stimulating ideas are pieces of costume. Such garments as hats, capes, aprons, shawls, tailcoats, and jewelry will suggest different kinds of characters. Innumerable examples could be given of situations that grew from characters developed this way. For example, to one boy, a tailcoat suggested a musician, down on his luck and playing his violin on a street corner for pennies. A feathered hat helped a little girl create a lady of fashionable pretensions, and become a comic character in her extravagant dress and poor taste. A shawl has suggested witches, grandmothers, people in disguise, or a scene laid in very cold weather.

It is wise for the teacher on any level, working anywhere, to keep a supply of simple and sturdy costumes available for this kind of use. If children experience difficulty in getting into character, a piece of a costume may sometimes be all that is needed to provide the necessary incentive. Costume used in this way is not dressing the part, but an aid to more imaginative thinking.

IMPROVISATION FROM CHARACTERS

In an earlier chapter, an illustration was given of an improvisation created from a character. This is a successful method of starting, as well as a way of encouraging observation. If the group is small and has had some experience, original monologues are good practice and fun for the players. If the class is large, however, this is probably not a wise assignment, unless the monologues are kept short.

To create from a character, the teacher can ask each member of the class to think of a particularly interesting person he has noticed that day, or sometime during the week. This is followed by questions as to:

Who was he?
What was he doing?

Did he have anything to say?
How did he dress?
How old was he?
What special thing about him attracted your attention?

One girl offered as a character a woman who served the hot vegetables in her school cafeteria. Although the woman was bad-tempered, the girl had observed that she was always extremely generous in her servings and did her job more efficiently than anyone else. The group, which chose her as a heroine for their story, decided that she might have been a refugee. Because she had experienced hunger during that period in her life, she was determined that all plates would be generously filled, now that food was available. Her irritability they attributed to her own unhappy experiences and her separation from her family. The scene that the children improvised, using this particular character as an inspiration, was thoughtful, sympathetic, and interesting to the class.

Another improvisation based on an actual person was the story of an elderly woman whom one child noticed every day, sitting on the front porch of her house. The group, who chose her for a heroine, decided that she was really very rich, but miserly, and was saving her money for the day when her son came home. They agreed that he had gone into the army several years before and had not returned. Although he had been reported missing, his mother clung to the hope that he would come back some day, and so she sat on the porch—waiting by day, and counting her money by night. The group decided to have him return, so the story had a happy ending.

A fantasy was the result of another character study. Two of the children described a well-dressed old man, whom they saw coming home every morning around eight o'clock. They decided that he must have an interesting occupation and so made him a wizard, who helped the good people and punished the evil through the power of his magic cane. This became a modern fairy tale filled with highly imaginative incidents.

IMPROVISATIONS FOR TWO

Try to imagine yourself in the following situations:

1. You receive a letter in the mail, telling you that you have won first prize in a poster contest. Tell your mother the good news.
2. Your dog has been hit by a car. When you come home from school, your mother meets you and tells you what has happened.
3. You become separated from your mother while shopping in a large department store. You find someone who you think can help you.
4. You are trying on shoes to take to camp. The clerk does not have what you want and tries to sell you something else. Should you take his suggestion?
5. You are moving to a new neighborhood today. Your best friend comes around to say goodbye to you. Although you are looking forward to your new home, you are sad to leave the old neighborhood. What do you say?
6. Your aunt, whom you have never met, has come for a visit. You answer the door. What is she like? What do you say to each other?
7. You have found a kitten that you want very much to keep, but your mother has said you cannot have a pet. Try to persuade her that the kitten needs a home.
8. A salesman comes to the door. He insists on demonstrating a vacuum cleaner, although you tell him you have one. How do you handle the situation?
9. You have been wanting ice skates for your birthday. Your grandmother, who always selects the right presents, comes to the door with a box in her hands. When you open it, you find it contains stationery. What do you say to each other?
10. You wore your sister's bracelet on a picnic, and when you get home, discover you have lost it. Now you must tell her what happened.

EXERCISES FOR THREE

1. You and your friend are going to the playground. Your little sister wants to go with you, but if she does, you cannot go into the area reserved for older children. What do you do?

2. You are delivering papers. You throw one toward a house, but instead of landing on the porch, it breaks a window. Both the man and his wife come to see what has happened.
3. You and your friend find a five-dollar bill on the sidewalk. You want to keep it, but at this moment a woman comes down the street looking for something. You are certain she has lost it. What do you do?
4. You tried out for a leading part in a play but were put in the chorus. You try to be a good sport when you talk to the teacher, and to the girl who was cast in the part you wanted.
5. Your mother has just given your old rag doll to your younger cousin, who is visiting you. Neither of them knows how much the doll means to you. You try to pretend it is all right.

OTHER SUGGESTIONS

Unfinished stories can also be used to stimulate thinking. If the teacher introduces a character and sets the scene, the group is given the problem of completing the story. Although this is more an exercise in plotting, the action is motivated by the character: an interesting character makes for an interesting plot.

One club group showed an unusual interest in holidays, so the teacher used this as a springboard for the entire year. She brought in stories about Halloween, Thanksgiving, Christmas, New Year's Day, Valentine's Day, St. Patrick's Day, April Fool's Day, Memorial Day, and the Fourth of July. Sometimes the group acted out the stories she read to them; sometimes they made up stories of their own, suggested by the occasion. One day they observed that there was no holiday in August. The result was an original play, which they called *A Holiday for August.* It was to be a festival of children's games, which developed into a particularly attractive summer pageant. August was the narrator, who began by telling of his disappointment that no one had ever thought to put a holiday in his month. At the conclusion, he expressed his joy that the children had made him special with a festival of games played in his honor.

IMPROVISATIONS BASED ON STORIES

The most popular and, in many ways, most satisfactory form of improvisation for children is based on good stories. While making up original stories is a creative exercise, a group endeavor rarely achieves the excellence of a story that has stood the test of time, or has been written by a fine author. This is a way of introducing literature, and when it is well chosen, offers good opportunities for acting. Chapters Six and Seven illustrate the ways in which both simple and more complicated stories have been approached.

Good stories on any level should have literary quality, worthwhile ideas, correct information, and dramatic values. Children up to the age of ten and eleven like fairy tales and legends. Older children may still enjoy these but tend to prefer adventure, biography, and stories of real life. Frequently the latter, because of their length, will have to be cut, or the incidents rearranged. This is a learning experience, which, if the group has had some experience, should not be too difficult.

Sometimes groups will want to act plays they have seen. When the experience has been a good one, this can be a worthwhile activity, though the tendency is to try to do it exactly as it was presented on the stage. Nevertheless, it can be a valuable period of time spent with a good piece of literature, and is to be preferred to the reproduction of television shows or enactment of stories from comic books.

In order to present the right story, the leader must, first of all, know the group well. One leader, who was later to achieve remarkable success, told of her first experience as a young teacher at a settlement house in a disadvantaged urban area. Nothing she brought to the children in her drama group captured their interest. Improvisation seemed an impossible goal, though the group was alert and lively when she saw them on the street. Finally she hit upon the idea of asking them to tell her stories they knew. Hesitantly at first, then willingly, legends and anecdotes came. She tried them. Not only was the material a success—the group doubled in size. Parents began to look in. Before the end of the year, an activity, which had seemed doomed to failure, became the most popular in the settlement. Some years later, the Drama Department was to achieve nationwide recognition as an arts center. The search for material had led to the children themselves. Their cultural heritage, and creative use of it under intelligent and sensitive guidance, was the first step.

The leader should prepare for improvisation of the story in advance, but avoid any preconceived ideas as to how it should be done. Improvisation is a group project with ideas contributed by both children and leader. The teacher is ready to offer suggestions but must be equally receptive to those of the players.

He should not expect the product to be perfect. Improvisation is never twice the same, and while repetition usually leads to greater fluency and richness of detail, each performance does not necessarily "top" the preceding one.

PUPPETRY

Although puppetry, as an art, merits a book in itself, it must be mentioned here as another, and excellent, medium of expression. Many teachers discover that children can often respond through puppets when they are unable to perform themselves. The puppet, an extension of the self, serves as a mask, enabling the player to gain a freedom which he cannot achieve when acting a part. Behind the puppet stage, the timid child can lose his inhibitions and enter into the drama without self-consciousness. Puppetry, therefore, is a valuable medium when:

1. The players are self conscious.
2. The room is inadequate for free movement.
3. The teacher knows something about puppetry or is able to work with the art department in the making of puppets.
4. The children themselves cannot move.

The last point is illustrated by the work of a young man who worked with bedridden children in a hospital. He devised stages for each bed so that the children could play stories together, with each child manipulating his own puppet. Though this would come in the category of creative dramatics for the handicapped, it is cited as an example of an imaginative approach to a problem that many teachers would have pronounced impossible.

Hand puppets are the most popular in schools, and simple ones can be constructed by quite young children. A puppet stage and puppets that function have many of the values of creative drama. Dialogue is not memorized, and the players must be thoroughly acquainted with their material in order to present it. Puppetry is a highly creative activity, in that not only the drama but the puppets themselves are made by the players.

The values in puppetry might be listed as follows:

1. Puppets provide opportunities for developing skills. Tools and materials must be handled with care in order to construct puppets that are sturdy and functional.
2. Dressing and decorating puppets require imagination. Each puppet must become a character, first through the costume it is given, and then in the way in which it is decorated, or painted.
3. Puppets require control. It takes controlled fingers to manipulate a puppet so that it can perform as the operator wishes.
4. Puppets offer an avenue of expression. Through the puppet, the operator expresses the thoughts and feelings of a character.
5. Puppets have therapeutic power. The timid or withdrawn child can find release through the puppet, whereas the aggressive child must learn to subordinate himself to the personality of the character he is presenting.
6. Puppets demand cooperation. Children learn to take turns and work together for a successful performance.
7. Puppetry is inexpensive. Delightful results may be obtained within the most limited budget. If there is no stage, a box will do until the teacher is able to construct something more permanent.

ROLE-PLAYING

Although it was stated in the first chapter that role-playing as therapy is not the job of the creative dramatics teacher, or the classroom teacher using creative dramatics techniques, some teachers have tried it with reported success. The purpose is educative rather than therapeutic, and the situations examined are common to all. Human conflicts and the ways in which problems are solved can promote social growth. Family scenes, school situations, and playground incidents give opportunity for interaction and group discussion. Discussion is the most important aspect of role-playing, according to some teachers, for it is during these periods that various points of view are presented and attitudes clarified. The teacher must accept all ideas, giving the boys and girls a chance to express themselves without fear of disapproval. He will pose such questions as:

How do you think the father felt? The brother? The mother?
What did the man next door think when you broke his window?
How do you think he felt the third time it happened?
If you were he, how would you feel?

Exchanging roles is a good way to put oneself in the shoes of another, in order to understand him. One teacher gave a demonstration of role-playing done with her group of junior high school girls, who lived in a neighborhood with a growing Puerto Rican population. The girls had had difficulty in accepting the newcomers, and the teacher's introduction of role-playing, as a way of helping them understand the problem, led to the following improvisation. The scene was the planning of a school dance by a small clique. The committee wished to exclude the newcomers but could accomplish it only by making them feel unwelcome. This led to a serious breakdown in group relations. The period spent in playing the situation reportedly did much to restore peace and communication. The problem was faced squarely, and the girls were able to discuss their own attitudes and feelings. Later on, when the improvisation was done as a demonstration for a university class, it made a tremendous impression. The insights expressed through the honesty of the players proved the value of the experiment. The teacher did not claim to be a therapist, but was an intelligent and experienced classroom teacher, who was deeply troubled about a condition that was interfering with the work of the class.

Peter Slade, in *Child Drama,* summarizes the use of role-playing in this way: "I would go so far as to say that one of the most important reasons for developing child drama in schools generally is not actually a therapeutic one but the even more constructive one of prevention." [1]

It must be pointed out that playing the part of a fictional character also demands identification with him and his problems. Exchange of parts gives all of the players a chance to experience both sides of a conflict. Obviously, the conflict which the group itself experiences is stronger, and the solution, if found, is of practical benefit.

SUMMARY

In summary, improvisation is the creation of a situation in which characters speak spontaneously. There are many ways of introducing improvisation, but some ground work in pantomime is the best preparation. Once the players have achieved a sense of security in movement, they are ready to add dialogue. Dialogue does not come easily at first, but continued practice on familiar material usually induces the flow. There are many points of departure, and some of the most successful are those described in this chapter: improvisation from situations; objects or properties; sounds; characters; ideas and stories. A good program is one that makes use of all, though the teacher will be flexible in his approach, using those methods which lead to the greatest success for his group. Stories should be chosen with care, and include both familiar and new material. Although the leader will probably want to start

---

1. Peter Slade, *Child Drama* (London: University of London Press, 1954), p. 119.

with the known, he will find this an excellent opportunity to widen horizons by bringing in good literature with dramatic content.

Role-playing is a kind of improvisation, which has as its specific objective the social growth of the individuals. There may well be a place for it in the school or club program but it must not be confused with creative dramatics as art. Both, however, are participant-centered, and in that respect differ from theatre. When observed by others, improvised drama of any kind should be considered as demonstration and not as performance.

There is a great interest in improvisation today, and several professional theatre groups specialize in it. This, like the *commedia dell' arte* of the sixteenth century, is the development of improvisational theatre by adult actors to a high level of artistry. While many boys and girls are able to become involved in the playing, the purpose of improvisation with children is not to entertain but rather to provide them with a medium of self-expression. The leader, or teacher, whether working in school, camp, or club program, tries to stimulate the imagination, free the individual to create, guide the group, and build confidence. Evaluating the results with the group ultimately leads to richer performance and personal growth.

CHAPTER 5

Dramatic Structure: The Play Takes Shape

If a creative dramatics teacher is going to help children create a play, he must know something of the structure and fundamental dramatic elements that distinguish the play from other forms of literature. He will not be expected to become expert at playwriting or dramatic criticism, but his enjoyment will be greater, and his guidance more helpful, if he has a basic understanding of the art form with which he is working. While there is no established formula for writing a play, particularly in this period of experimentation, there are certain elements that are necessary to its existence.

First of all, a play is to be played. Until it finds life upon a stage, it is not a play. Through the process of interpretation by actors, and the mounting by costume and scenic designers, it is born; and it will live or die according to the communication it has for an audience. It is true that some plays have been popular in their own times but have failed to speak to subsequent generations of playgoers. Occasionally, but much less often, a play that is badly received when it opens finds an audience later. All too often, however, the play that fails to please in its first production is discarded before there is another opportunity to tell whether or not it communicates with even a limited audience.

There are plays that are universal and timeless in their appeal; what they have to say is as true today as when they were written, and this truth is understood by men of all races and national backgrounds. There are other plays, however, whose messages are more temporal. Couched in the language of the day, they speak to the men of their own times, presenting problems both serious and comic, to which contemporary audiences respond, but to which those of another time or place are indifferent. This is not to discredit such plays but simply to observe that, as theatre pieces, they have found success but lack the universality and timelessness of the classics. What will come out of our own time must be left to future generations of playgoers to decide. The works of George Bernard Shaw, Eugene O'Neill, and Tennessee Williams are among those that have been translated into many languages and produced widely both at home and abroad. It is too soon to tell, however, to whom they will speak in the future.

Styles in playwriting change. Both the times and the theatres for which they are written affect the structure; nevertheless, there are certain elements that identify the drama as a specific art form.

CHARACTERS

A play involves characters. It is their conflict that holds our attention, and it is through them that the playwright delivers his message. Whether tragic or comic, lovable or despised, a character must be believable and belong to the play. Even in fantasy, a character must have reality; a witch or a ghost, for example, though unrealistic in itself, must compel our belief through the consistency of its behavior.

The hero or heroine should be someone with whom the audience can identify. Whatever his faults or human weaknesses, he must arouse our sympathy, making us care what happens to him. Whether he should be more good than bad is debatable, but we must accept him as real, and his actions as true.

Characters react to each other in a natural way. Though it is clearly established to whom the story belongs, there are other characters in the play who help to advance the plot through their involvement with it and their relationship to the hero, or protagonist. A skillful playwright develops character and situation through this interaction. Sometimes many characters are needed to tell a story; sometimes it is done better with one or two. The fewer there are, the greater the responsibility they have for telling the story, and the more the audience learns about them. The actor, however, must find in the most minor character the answers or clues to such questions as:

1. The age of the character.
2. His education and cultural background.
3. His interests.
4. His occupation or profession.
5. His religion.
6. The members of his family and his relationship to them.
7. His social relationships.
8. His physical appearance and health.
9. His dominant mood.
10. His qualities of personality.

Good characters are at all times consistent. If they are not, either through the writing or the actor's interpretation, we cannot believe in them. A believable character, on the other hand, has a reality that exists for the audience long after the final curtain has been drawn.

DIALOGUE

Dialogue is the term given to the lines of the play. Good dialogue should belong to the characters, both in content and manner of speech. A nobleman will not talk like a peasant, nor will a country boy talk like a prince. While dialogue must, of course, be understood, the speech patterns of the characters must not be sacrificed. For example, a character of little education, who comes from a particular region, will use colloquial speech or appropriate dialect. Poetic dialogue has been employed during certain periods of history, but even this convention does not obscure the speech patterns and individuality of the characters.

Dialogue advances the plot. The playwright's job is to tell the story as economically as possible through the words of his characters. A soliloquy, in which only one person speaks, is a device occasionally used, but, in general, it is through conversation between two or more persons that characters are revealed and the plot is unfolded.

PLOT

The plot is the story. It may be simple or complex, internal or external, but what happens between the opening scene and the final curtain is the action we call story or plot. While tastes differ and styles change, a good plot holds the interest of the audience and is consistent. The most bizarre events must belong to it; and the outcome, whatever it may be, must seem logical.

CONFLICT

Conflict is the basis of drama, whether comic or tragic. Without conflict, there is no resolution; with conflict, the interest is sustained to the end. The successful playwright resolves the conflict in a way that is satisfying and acceptable.

THEME

The theme is the underlying thought or basic idea upon which the play rests. Not every play has a well-defined theme; it may, however, be the most important element. If there is a theme, the story both springs from and expresses it.

CLIMAX

The climax is the high point of the play. A three- or five-act play will have more than one climax but there will always be a point at which the interest of the audience is highest. This scene usually comes somewhere near the end, after which there is an untangling, or resolution.

DENOUEMENT

This is the portion of the play that follows the climax. It may be long or short, depending upon the number of situations that need straightening out. In a children's play, the denouement and climax are often one, since children are satisfied once the conflict is settled, and long explanations at this point do not interest them.

UNITY

This is the overall term applied to the integration of the various parts of the drama, making a smooth and consistent whole. Unity may be achieved in a number of ways, such as the creation of: a single hero, a single action, a single idea, a single mood. On the other hand, a good play, no matter how many characters or episodes, can also be unified through the sensitive arrangement and organization of the various parts.

DRAMATIC IRONY

Dramatic irony is the term used for letting the audience in on a secret. Suspense is usually greater when it is employed, and many comedy scenes are funnier because of it.

STRUCTURE

Plays are described as long or short depending on whether they are a full evening's entertainment or consist of merely one act. The number of acts in a long play varies. Though many playwrights have used the three-act form, some prefer four or five, or a series of episodes, rather than the conventional division between acts. Scenes are the divisions within acts, and usually occur when the time or place changes.

COMEDY

Comedy is defined as a play that ends satisfactorily for the hero or heroine. Comedy may be funny, but this is not essential according to the definition. Many comedies are serious, or satiric.

TRAGEDY

Tragedy is defined as a play that ends with the death or defeat of the leading character. Though fashions change, and violence and death are not currently popular, the downfall of the hero places the play in the category of tragedy.

PROLOGUE AND EPILOGUE

These are the portions of the play sometimes placed at the beginning and end, to introduce it, or to establish atmosphere. Such scenes are not an integral part of the play, though a narrator may appear in the prologue and also be involved in the plot. Many children's plays employ narrators, or are written with prologues as a means of imparting necessary information to an audience composed of different age levels and theatre experience.

CHILDREN'S THEATRE

Children's theatre is first and foremost good theatre. In this respect, it does not differ from theatre for adults. There are, however, special requirements that must be met if the children's play is to hold their interest as well as be worthy of their time and attention. The script contains the same basic elements—characters, dialogue, plot—but not all material appropriate to the adult audience is suitable for children. Action, for example, is particularly important: the playwright, writing for children, must remember that it is more important to "show" than to "tell." Speeches should be short; long, talky dialogue is lost on the audience. Though vocabulary is necessarily adapted to the age level of the audience, it should not be oversimplified but should, rather, add enrichment and an opportunity for learning new words.

In writing an adaptation of a classic or well-known story, the playwright must make every effort to retain the essential elements of the source material so as not to disappoint or offend his audience. Characters must be believable. Fantasy and fairy stories comprise a large segment of plays written for children; nevertheless, the characters in such plays must be endowed with credibility, exhibiting a pattern of behavior that is consistent.

If the playwright has suggested difficult technical problems, he must ask himself whether they can be carried out successfully, or whether any modification of the effect will damage the play. By technical problems are meant such things as blackouts; characters who fly, disappear, or change into birds or animals; or unusual lighting and sound effects. What might be easily solved in the professional theatre can often pose an insoluble problem on the school stage, where equipment, budget, and technical assistance are limited.

Children's theatre, like adult theatre, should not depend on extravagant effects or gimmicks to stimulate interest; if such scenes are essential to the plot, however, and can be executed artistically, they will certainly add to the effectiveness. Children do not demand theatricality, but there is no question that their enjoyment is enhanced by scenes that offer excitement and color.

VALUES

Much has been said about the values of theatre for children and basic to it is, of course, the script. The children's playwright has a special and difficult task, since he cannot anticipate the age level that will be attending his play. The chances are that his audience will range from five to twelve, perhaps a span even greater. Efforts have been made in some communities to try to control the age of the audience, either by a statement in the publicity, or by two series of plays. This persists as a problem, however, and is one with which the playwright is faced.

Children's interests change, as has been mentioned. While fairy and animal tales are popular with younger children, the eleven- or twelve-year-old prefers adventure, history, biography, and stories of real life. The attention span of the older child is longer, hence he can be absorbed for as long as two hours, in contrast to the younger child, who can probably not give full attention for more than one.

To the younger child, a character is all good or all bad. As he grows older, he begins to comprehend motives and can see a combination of faults and virtues, or weakness and strength, in a single person. Children identify with characters of high motives and brave deeds. Through this experience they grow, and gain appreciation for the ideals and standards by which men live. Values, therefore, are important to both young and old. Material that confirms such values as honesty, integrity, and social concern holds the interest of all, and may be presented without condescension.

In our preoccupation with ideals and values, we sometimes forget the appeal that comedy holds. Children of all ages love humor, though what is funny to the younger child—riddles, jokes, repetition, slapstick, the chase—does not appeal to his older brother or sister. Comical characters, ridiculous situations, and amusing lines are the materials of comedy, and may even teach more effectively than the serious play. Some of our social critics have used comedy to point up the defects and flaws of society.

Some criticism has been directed at those playwrights and producers who give children only the musical play. This seems to be a trend of the times, with the adult theatre having an equally large portion. However, whatever the medium—if the ingredients of taste and credibility are combined with a worthwhile idea, a hero with whom the audience can identify, action, poetic justice, and literary quality, the playwright will have accomplished his purpose.

The Three Wishes

The following script of *The Three Wishes* is included as an illustration of a well-known children's story that contains all the elements of a play:

A worthwhile and relevant theme.
A plot that holds interest.
Plenty of action.
Characters who motivate the action.
Conflict.
Humor.
A definite climax and satisfactory end.

Like most old tales, *The Three Wishes* may be enjoyed by a wide age range, though it is better improvised by children under twelve. Despite the magic, it can be produced simply in classroom, club room, or camp. Producing the sausages and making them hang from Joanna's nose is a challenge to ingenuity but it is not a difficult problem to solve. The business of the sausages, incidentally, provides excellent material for pantomime or improvisation, and it is suggested that this part be played by itself, before actual rehearsals begin.

THE THREE WISHES

(An Old Tale)

Joanna (An old peasant woman)
Peter (Her husband)
A stranger (A young man with an air of mystery about him)

(The scene is a small cottage. In the room are a table, chairs, a cupboard, and a fireplace. Down right there is a door leading to the outside. As the curtain rises, Joanna, an old woman with a discontented expression on her face, is sweeping the hearth.)

JOANNA: As if I could ever sweep all the dust and dirt from the hearth with this broom. (*She examines it.*) As many twigs fall from it as I have swept up. The old man will have to make me another, if he expects me to keep the house clean. (*She sweeps again for a moment, then stops and leans on the broom.*) Or better yet, if we had a servant girl, she could do all the cleaning. Think how that would be! To do nothing all day like our neighbor but sit in a chair by the fire and watch someone else do the work. Oh, why has the old man never earned enough to keep just one servant girl? Not five like the Duke. Nor four like our neighbor. Not even two like the simplest farmer. But one. Just one servant girl would be all I'd ask. (*She sighs.*) Oh, well, if the good man has not made his fortune yet he never will now. And we'll end our lives just as we began them—poor peasants in a cottage. (*She puts the broom in a corner and begins to set the table for supper. While she is doing this, Peter, her husband, comes in. He steps wearily through the doorway, then stops, leaning on a stout stick.*)

PETER: (*Sniffs*) What! Supper not on the table? What have you been doing all day while I worked in the fields?

JOANNA: What do you expect with no one to help me? If we had a servant girl now, the supper would be ready and waiting.

PETER: And if I had a donkey to carry the plough, I'd not be so tired. I could climb on his back when the day's work was done and ride home in comfort.

JOANNA: A donkey? Why not wish for a horse? We could get a cart then and both of us drive out together on Sunday.

PETER: (*Sitting by the hearth and continuing eagerly*) Yes, a strong brown horse like our neighbor's. I'd want one like his. Then I could plant a garden that brought in some money. In time I could buy another horse. With a team there's no telling how much we could earn.

JOANNA: Well, we haven't even one donkey. So pull up your chair and I'll have supper on the table in a minute.

PETER: (*Sitting at the table*) Cabbage soup again?

JOANNA: (*Bringing the pot to the table and ladeling out the soup*) What did you expect? Meat and white bread like the Duke? Cabbage is the only thing in the garden.

PETER: (*Eating it hungrily*) It's good. Though it would be better if you'd had a bone to cook with it.

JOANNA: A bone means meat. When have we had a roast with a bone left to flavor the soup?
(*She sits down and tastes her soup. Then she takes a piece of bread.*) White bread now, instead of black. That would help.

PETER: White bread with butter, eh, wife?

JOANNA: (*Eagerly*) When I stopped at our neighbor's today with the basket of cabbages to sell, I caught a glimpse of the kitchen. Such things as they were fixing for dinner! Cakes, butter, cream, and a goose roasting on the spit.

PETER: Ah, well, we are poor folk, Joanna. We could wish till the end of our days and nothing would come of it.
(*At this moment a voice is heard from the fireplace.*)

STRANGER: Nothing would come of it? Are you sure, Peter? Are you sure, Joanna?

PETER: Who was that?

JOANNA: Was that you, Peter?

PETER: (*Getting up*) I'd swear I heard a voice.

STRANGER: (*Coming out of the fireplace*) And so you did. (*He brushes off his clothes.*) Now, then, what was that you were saying?

PETER: (*Startled*) Oh, nothing. Nothing important.

STRANGER: Come, now, Peter, Joanna. You were wishing for a well-stocked larder, I think.

JOANNA: Well, yes, we were.

STRANGER: Are you sure that's all that you wish for?

PETER: (*Eagerly*) Oh, no. If I had a donkey now—

JOANNA: Not a donkey, Peter, a horse. So we could ride in a carriage together.

PETER: And plough a garden that went from here to that forest.

STRANGER: I'll tell you what. I've been listening to the two of you for some time and I'm about to make you a gift.

PETER: What kind of a gift?

JOANNA: Who are you? And how did you come here?

STRANGER: Let's say I'm a stranger who heard you in passing. (*He walks around the table and they look at him in wonder.*) Oh, I'm not a rich man, if that's what you're thinking. Though I do have strange powers.

PETER: What kind of powers?

STRANGER: I'll show you. Yes, I'm going to give you three wishes.

PETER: (*Repeating the words after him, stupidly*) Three wishes?

STRANGER: Yes. But I must warn you, you'll have only three wishes between you. So watch out you don't waste them.

PETER: (*Joyfully*) You mean, if I wished for a donkey, I'd get one?

JOANNA: No, Peter, a horse, not a donkey.

STRANGER: Sh! That's what I mean. Be careful. When you've used the three wishes up, there'll be no more of them. Think of what you want most.

PETER: And they'll be granted, no matter how great the request?

STRANGER: They'll be granted, never fear. But only the three. So watch out, Peter.
(*The stranger moves back to the hearth and disappears as the old couple talk excitedly together.*)

PETER: Did you hear that, Joanna? Why, I can wish for a team of horses with a carriage to boot!

JOANNA: And a house!

PETER: Or a castle! With a kitchen as big as this room.

JOANNA: Filled with all sorts of good things to eat. (*She turns to speak to the Stranger.*) Must we use all three wishes at once or can we save one for— Why, where has he gone? He's not here, Peter.

PETER: (*Rubbing his eyes*) Vanished as suddenly as he appeared. Do you suppose we just dreamed this?

JOANNA: No, of course not. How could we both dream the same thing? And at the same time? He must have gone out the door while we were talking. Let's go after him.
(*The two old people go quickly to the door but do not see him.*)

JOANNA: He's nowhere in sight. You go down the road, Peter. He may have gone round the bend.

PETER: All right. (*He disappears from sight, calling.*) Hey, hey, there!

JOANNA: Gone before we even had a chance to thank him. He was standing right here. (*Puzzled, she stands in the middle of the room for a moment.*) We might have asked him to supper. I wish we'd—(*She claps her hands over her mouth.*) Just in time. Now, then, what to wish for?
(*Peter comes in the door and goes to his chair.*)

PETER: Not a sign of him anywhere. You don't think, wife—

JOANNA: That we only imagined him? No, I don't. He said he had magic powers. Therefore, why couldn't he disappear like smoke in the breeze? (*She has an idea.*) Up the chimney, perhaps? (*She goes to the hearth and looks up the chimney.*)

JOANNA: Not there, either. Come, Peter. Let's sit down and think of three things to wish for.

PETER: Well, I still think a horse would be—

JOANNA: Sh! Remember what he said. Don't wish till we've thought of everything we need. I'd say a house, instead of this cottage.

PETER: Or a castle with barns—

JOANNA: And servants—

PETER: And fine dresses for you—

JOANNA: And a gold-headed cane for you to lean on when you're tired.

PETER: Wait! We can't waste a wish on a cane. Why not wish me young and strong again? Then I'd have no use for a cane.

JOANNA: (*Excited*) Both of us young again, Peter! As we were when we first moved into this cottage. My hair would be black. And when I put on my fine clothes, I'd be as beautiful as the Duke's daughter.

PETER: We mustn't be hasty. Let's eat our soup and then after supper, we'll decide. (*He takes a spoonful of soup.*) It's cold.

JOANNA: And why shouldn't it be? Sitting out in these bowls. (*She takes a spoonful.*) Oh, I wish we had sausage to go with it. (*No sooner has she said the words than a sausage is on her plate.*)

PETER: Oh, Joanna, see what you've done! Only two wishes left!

JOANNA: I didn't mean to do it.

PETER: (*Angrily*) You've thrown away one third of our fortune, Joanna. I wish that sausage were on the end of your nose!

(*At once the sausage is hanging from her nose. She puts her hands up and feels it.*)

JOANNA: Peter!

PETER: I'm sorry, Joanna. I was angry. I didn't think. Here, let me pull it off.

JOANNA: It's stuck tight. I'm trying.

PETER: (*Going over to her, he pulls and pulls.*) It certainly seems to be stuck there. Come, let's both pull.
(*They both pull but the sausage refuses to budge.*)
It seems as if the harder we pull, the faster it sticks. I have it! I'll cut it off.

JOANNA: No, Peter. You might cut my nose.
(*Peter gets a huge knife and comes toward her.*)

PETER: I'll be careful. Let me try.

JOANNA: (*Running away from him*) No, no. Leave me alone.

PETER: Perhaps if I cut it off just below—about here?

JOANNA: I don't want even half a sausage on the end of my nose. (*Wailing*) Oh, Peter, what shall I do?

PETER: Just one wish left. Shall it be a house or the horses and carriage?

JOANNA: I can't go about with a sausage hanging on my nose. No matter how rich we were, people would laugh.

PETER: You could tie a scarf over your face.

JOANNA: Every time I stepped out of the house?

PETER: Perhaps no one would notice—

JOANNA: Oh, Peter, how would you like to have a sausage hanging down over your chin?

PETER: It may go away.

JOANNA: It won't, I know. Oh, Peter, there's just one thing to do.

PETER: You mean—

JOANNA: Yes. To wish it off. Are you willing?

PETER: I guess you're right. (*They look at each other.*) We were both foolish.

PETER }
JOANNA }: (Together) We wish the sausage off her/my nose. (*Miraculously the sausage comes off in Joanna's hand.*)

JOANNA: There. (*Sadly*) All three wishes gone. And we're no better off than we were.

PETER: Except, perhaps— Come, wife, let us eat our supper and be grateful that no more harm was done. After all, we do have soup in our bowls—

JOANNA: And a roof over our heads—

PETER: And strength enough to work in the fields.

JOANNA: And each other.

PETER: And, who knows, perhaps some day he will come again. The next time—(*He and Joanna look at each other and laugh.*)

(THE CURTAIN FALLS)

Costumes The costumes may be of any period or national background since the tale appears in the folklore of several countries. Joanna and Peter are peasants, and their clothes should suggest this.

Scenery	table	fireplace
	2 chairs	cupboard
Properties	broom	ladle
	stick	2 spoons
	2 plates	loaf of brown bread
	2 soup bowls	string of sausages
	large soup pot	

A floor plan is suggested but the playing space and location of entrances may make another arrangement more desirable. It is simple enough to be played anywhere.

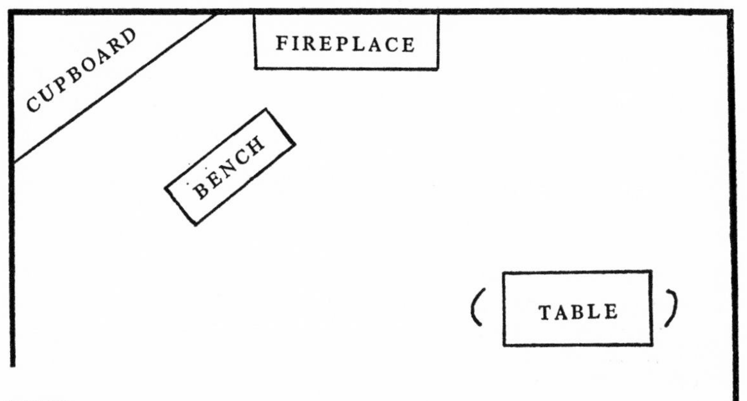

NOTE: The sausages pose the only technical problem in this play. There are a variety of ways of handling it, but it is suggested that they be made a of a lightweight material such as nylon stockings, filled with cotton and tied together at intervals to form links. Masking tape, adhesive tape, nose putty, or any material that has an adhesive quality must be put on one end so that they stick tight. In appearing to pull them, Joanna must see that they stay on, and Peter must watch that he does not knock them off. While seeming to tug at them, Joanna can actually be holding them firmly in place. If she turns slightly when they appear and disappear, she will prevent the audience from seeing how the magic is performed.

CHAPTER 6

Building Plays From Simple Stories

When the group has had some experience with pantomime and improvisation, it will be ready to attempt a story. Groups of all ages welcome this next step and often have suggestions of their own to offer regarding favorite stories or material from other classes which they want to dramatize. Regardless of how well they may know the story, there is still some preliminary work to be done before improvisation begins. The teacher, well acquainted with the group by this time, knows the kind of material that will have an appeal and present the fewest difficulties. Success is important to future work, and the leader will want to select a story that he is relatively sure the group can handle.

There is a wealth of good literature readily available, which both group and leader can enjoy and find worthy of their efforts. The stories and poems included in this and the two following chapters is illustrative of the kinds of material that groups of all ages have used successfully. Suggestions are offered as to ways in which it may be presented and handled. It should not be inferred that these are the only or even the best ways of using the material; they are merely illustrations of the thinking done by some groups.

Folk tales, legends, and fables are recommended material for use on all levels, though different age groups view them in respect to their own maturity and experience. For younger children, stories should be simplified in the telling, whereas in working with older children, greater emphasis can be given to characterization. Meanings and insights come with experience as well as age; hence a really good story spans many age levels.

When the teacher has decided upon an appropriate story, he must decide whether it is better told, or read. In general, telling the story is preferable because it establishes a closer rapport with the audience, and gives the leader a chance to observe the listeners' reactions, and clarify, as he goes along, any points that appear to puzzle them. This means that he must be thoroughly familiar with the material; in fact, the beginning teacher will do well to practice telling the story aloud before he presents it to the group. This will add to his own self-confidence and help him develop greater variety and color in his presentation. A good voice and clear diction are certainly assets, but even more important is the teacher's ability to involve himself in the material so that the story comes alive to the listeners. He will probably find it easier to establish contact if he sits down, with his audience gathered closely around him.

Choice of words is important in storytelling. Often, certain words or phrases in the story are repeated a number of times and are so important that the teller will wish to use them. He will not otherwise try to memorize the story, for this usually leads to a stilted presentation and the risk of forgetting. Knowing the story so well that it can be told in one's own words is a far more satisfactory way of sharing it. Descriptive words create vivid pictures; for example, words that suggest seeing, hearing, tasting, smelling, and touching help the listener to become more deeply interested and involved. Some impersonation makes characters come alive, though the storyteller's aim is to guide interpretation rather than to establish patterns for characterization. Facial expressions and gestures add to the interest, but only if they are natural and spontaneous. They should not be memorized and set, or the spontaneity will suffer.

Experience in telling stories helps the teacher to avoid such pitfalls as forgetting parts and having to return to them out of sequence. He will soon learn to proceed in order, holding the climax until the end, including as many details as his listeners are able to handle, and as are necessary to the story. He will avoid condescension, and will adapt his vocabulary to the age and background of the group, taking advantage, at the same time, of opportunities to introduce new words and explain ideas that are strange or foreign. With a little practice, most leaders can develop an effective storytelling technique, which stimulates enthusiasm for dramatization.

After the story has been told, and all questions answered, the children are ready to begin planning how they will handle it. A discussion should include a review of the plot and descriptions of the characters. When the leader feels that the group has the details well in mind, he will suggest that they try playing it. Asking for volunteers is a good way of starting: this gives the stronger ones a chance to try it first, and the more timid an opportunity to become better acquainted with it before taking their turns. Casting is done on a voluntary basis the first two or three times. Later on, the leader may suggest that other children try various parts. For instance, he might say, "Lynne hasn't had a chance yet. How would you like to try the princess this time?" Or, "John has been the cobbler. Let's give Alan a chance to play it. And you, John, be one of the townsfolk." Or, "I know David has a strong voice. How about letting him be the giant?"

In other words, it is the development of each participant that concerns us. Later on, when the group is ready to play the story for the last time, the leader might suggest those children who have brought the greatest reality to each part, but this is as close as we come to formal, or type, casting.

The situation may be played any number of times, but the replaying should not be interpreted as rehearsal. It is hoped, of course, that with each playing, the story will gain in substance and depth; that there will be deeper insights; and that the participants will develop greater freedom and self-confidence. The discussions preceding and following each playing are important aspects of creative dramatics, for it is during these periods that some of the most creative thinking takes place. Some questions that might precede the first playing are:

1. What do we want to tell?
2. Who are the people?
3. What are these people really like?
4. What are they doing when we first meet them?
5. Where does the first scene take place?
6. What kind of a house do they live in?

After the scene has been played once, more specific questions can guide the discussion. These might be:

1. Did they tell the story?
2. What did you like about the opening scene?
3. Did the people show that they were excited? (Angry, unhappy, etc.)
4. When we play it again, can you think of anything that would improve it?
5. Was anything important left out?

In the course of a year, there are often delightful results, and both the leader and group may honestly wish to share them with others. There is no reason why this should not be done, provided public performance was not the original intention. More often, however, the initial results will be crude and superficial. Dialogue will be scanty, despite the most careful planning. To the experienced leader, this does not represent failure. It is an early stage in the development of the group, and may, at that point, indicate real progress. Acceptance of the effort, therefore, does not mean that the leader is satisfied to remain at this level but, rather, that he recognizes the efforts that have been made and is aware of the values to those who have taken part. As he works with the group, he will become more selective in what he accepts but, in the beginning, he will accept all ideas because they have been offered. It is important for every member to feel that his ideas are worthy of consideration. In time, even eight- and nine-year-olds will learn to distinguish between contributions that advance the play and those that distract, or have little to do with it.

The following stories have been chosen for inclusion here because of their simplicity. Most groups are familiar with them, and like them, and need only to be refreshed as to the details. The first, *Caps for Sale,* is popular with younger children, but equally interesting to older children, and even adults, because of the underlying theme. Very young children enjoy being monkeys, and like to take turns acting the Peddler. Older children, however, quickly see a parallel between human behavior and the behavior of monkeys, hence find in this simple tale a meaning worthy of their thought and effort. Although *Caps for Sale,* or *The Peddler and His Caps,* is very well known, a brief synopsis of the story is included.

CAPS FOR SALE

There was once a little old man who made caps. All year long he worked at them: red caps, pink caps, yellow caps, blue, green, and purple caps, caps with feathers and caps without. Every so often, when he had made a large enough number of caps to sell, he would put them in his pack and take them around to the villages. This particular morning he decided that he had plenty of caps to peddle, and since it was a very fine summer day, he took himself off. His cries of "Caps for Sale" roused the townsfolk, and soon many of them were trying on caps and selecting the ones they wanted to buy. Butchers, bakers, shoemakers, mothers, children, and even the mayor himself, gathered around the little Peddler, trying on caps and admiring their appearances. Finally, the mayor, who had found nothing to his liking, took off his cap and tossed it back to the Peddler, suggesting that he come again some other day. "Not today, Peddler. Come back another time."

Reluctantly, all of the townsfolk followed his example, echoing the mayor's words that he return another day. Realizing that he could sell no caps in this village, the little Peddler departed. Before long, he passed by the edge of a woods, and feeling very sleepy, decided to lie down and rest. Soon, however, he fell fast asleep, his hats lying on the grass beside him. Now it happened that this part of the woods was inhabited by a band of monkeys. Monkeys are curious little fellows, and finding the Peddler asleep under a tree, they decided to investigate the contents of his pack. First one, then another, cautiously approached. When they saw that the Peddler was wearing a cap on his head, the monkeys tried the caps on their own little heads. Then they scampered a distance away, chattering excitedly, for they were very much pleased with themselves. The sound of the chattering soon awakened the Peddler. He reached for his pack and was astonished to find it empty. Greatly puzzled, he looked about him to see where the caps might have gone. Suddenly he saw the monkeys. He called to them, pleasantly at first, and asked them to give back his caps. They only chattered, "Chee, chee, chee," pleasantly, in reply.

Then he shook his fist at them and demanded his caps, but they just shook their fists back. Angrily, he stamped his foot at them but they only stamped their little monkey feet at him in return. He begged, and they begged; he moved a few steps away, and they moved a few steps away. Suddenly it occurred to him that the monkeys were doing everything he did. With a sweeping gesture, he removed his own cap and tossed it to the ground at his feet. Immediately all of the monkeys removed their caps and threw them down to the Peddler. He gathered his caps up as quickly as possible, then made a low bow and thanked the monkeys for returning them. Chattering happily, the monkeys also bowed; each was pleased with the trick he thought he had played on the other.

When the leader has finished telling the story, he will be wise to review the plot to make certain that it is clearly understood. From here on, there are many ways of proceeding. He may ask where the story begins, and how many scenes the group sees in it. They may suggest two, three, four, or even five, though they usually come to the conclusion that three main scenes are necessary. These are:

1. The Peddler starts out on his travels.
2. He arrives in the village.
3. He stops to rest in the forest.

Some groups imagine a road running all around the room, with the three scenes laid in different areas. This enables the Peddler to move from one place to another, and gives him an opportunity to talk to himself as he walks along. Since no scenery is used in creative dramatics, such an arrangement is perfectly feasible. Incidentally, one advantage of a large room in dramatizing this story is the amount of freedom it provides the players: they are not limited by the rows of seats or traditional stage area. When playing in an auditorium, however, the succession of scenes will follow a more conventional pattern, unless there is an apron (area in front of the curtain) to accommodate some of the action.

In discussing how the Peddler's occupation might be introduced, one group may suggest that he have a wife with whom he can talk over his plans for the day at breakfast. Another group may give him a helper; another, a son; and still another may insist that he lives alone and so, has him talk to himself.

Whether or not his trip down the road is considered a separate scene depends on the importance the group attaches to it, but the next major scene is certainly the village in which the Peddler attempts to sell his caps. One of the advantages of a story of this sort is the opportunity for characterization afforded by the villagers. As any number of villagers may be included, there is an opportunity for many children to take part. The mayor is always a favorite, though other delightful characters may be created; a shoemaker, a mother, a small boy, a farmer, a young girl, and a milliner are examples. The playing of this scene will be long or short depending upon the characterizations and the fun the children have with it. Again, if a road is used to suggest the Peddler's travels, he will move along to a place designated as a part of the forest. If the group is small, the same children who were villagers can be monkeys. If the group is large, however, there is ample opportunity for others to play the monkeys. One of the best features of this particular story is the flexibility of the cast: whatever its size, the entire group can take part in it.

Regardless of age, children always respond to the monkeys, and the activity demanded by their antics is conducive to bodily freedom. There is such great opportunity for pantomime in the final scene that the leader might do well to begin with it, as a means of relaxing the group. By the time all have been monkeys, they are better prepared to begin on the story.

In this, and, indeed, in any story selected for dramatization, it is a good idea to work on small portions first rather than to attempt the entire story at once. No matter how well the children may know the material, it is quite another thing to improvise the scenes. Therefore, working on short bits, not necessarily in sequence, makes for more successful playing. In this respect, it is similar to rehearsing a play: the director does not attempt to run through the complete script until he has rehearsed each individual scene.

Fables are popular with some groups, though the obvious moral does not appeal to others. One advantage of a fable is its brevity. There is action as well as a quick and satisfying ending. There is little opportunity for character development, however, though some groups will fill in the plot with delightful and imaginative dialogue. The following is one fable that boys particularly enjoy.

THE BOY WHO CRIED WOLF

There was once a shepherd lad who went out to the fields each day with his flock. One day, growing tired of his lonely life, he decided to create some excitement. And so, when he was a distance from the village, he cried, "Wolf! Wolf!" The townsfolk, hearing his cries, dropped their chores and ran up the mountainside to help him. When they got there, however, the shepherd boy only laughed, and they realized the trick that had been played on them.

The following morning, the boy did the same thing again, and again the townsfolk ran to his rescue. Discovering that he had fooled them a second time, they returned to their work, angrily vowing that they would not be taken in by this trick again. On the third morning, when the boy was high up on the mountain, he heard a disturbance among the sheep. Seeing a wolf attacking them, he called out in terror. "Wolf! Wolf!" No one came. Again he called, "Wolf! Wolf! A wolf is attacking my sheep!"

The townsfolk heard his cries, but thinking it to be only a joke, did not go to his aid. The shepherd lad learned a lesson that day: if one cries "Wolf!" too often, no one comes when there really is danger.

The leader will not want to spend a great deal of time on this story since there is only one major character. On the other hand, the townsfolk offer opportunities for creating a variety of persons. Who are they? What is each doing when he hears the boy's cries, and what is his reaction when he discovers the trick? Who starts up the mountainside first? How would an old man feel if he climbed up a steep hillside for nothing? How does each one respond the second day? What does each say to his neighbor on the third morning? Such questions as these help the group create individual characters of the crowd.

Because the story is so short, every child can have a chance to try the part of the shepherd. What is he like? How do we know he is lonely and restless? Where are his sheep? How does he hit on the trick he plays? How does he feel when he sees the wolf? What does he do when the people fail to come to his rescue? Does he learn a lesson?

If there is a stage in the room, it may be used as the mountain where the sheep are grazing. If there is no stage, the boy can be at one end of the room so as to suggest the distance between him and the village. There is excitement in this story, and the kind of action that appeals to younger children. The lesson, incidentally, is one that all are able to understand and appreciate.

The Tortoise and the Hare is another fable that has great appeal, and may be played without much time spent in preparation. Although the characters are animals, children enjoy discovering what they can do to suggest their characteristics and give them reality.

THE TORTOISE AND THE HARE

There was once a Hare who was forever boasting of his great speed. In fact, whenever more than two animals gathered together in the forest, he would appear and then take the opportunity of telling them that he could outstrip the best of them. Stretching his long legs proudly, he would declare, "No one has ever beaten me. When I race at full speed, there is no one who can pass me."

The other animals said nothing, for there was no one who wished to dispute him. One day, the Tortoise, who had been listening quietly, replied, "I accept your challenge. I will race you."

"That is a good joke," laughed the Hare. "I could go to the goalpost and back before you had passed the first marker."

"Save your breath until you've won," said the Tortoise. "I'm willing to race you."

The other animals, who were mighty tired of listening to the Hare's boasts, were only too glad to hear someone speak up, though they secretly wished it had been an animal with a greater chance of winning. Nevertheless, they cheered the little Tortoise on and helped draw up a course. Then they lined up on each side and the Cock called the start of the race: 1—2—3—GO!

The Hare was gone and out of sight in a flash as his white cottontail disappeared through the bushes. The Tortoise kept his eyes straight ahead and never varied his pace. Presently, the Hare returned and danced around him, laughing at his slow progress. The Tortoise didn't say a word. Then, to show his scorn for the Tortoise, he lay down under a tree. He yawned, shut his eyes, and finally curled up and took his afternoon nap. The Tortoise only smiled and plodded on. After a while, the Hare awoke from his sleep. He opened his eyes just in time to see the Tortoise crawl past the winning post. As fast as he could make his legs go, he could not get there in time to save the race. The Tortoise, slow as he was, had crawled steadily forward while the Hare had spent his time running in circles and taking a nap. "I've learned a lesson today," said the Hare, ashamed of himself for having made so much fun of his opponent. "It's hard work, and not speed, that wins the race."

After the leader has told the fable, there is a good opportunity for total group participation: all can be hares, then tortoises. Younger children particularly enjoy the physical movement of this story. After some preliminary pantomime, it can be played in its entirety, since it is so short. A large room lends itself to the race, which may be run in a wide circle or in repeated circling of the space. Unless the group is very large, all may take turns playing the two parts, with the rest participating as the other animals watching the contest. This is a highly satisfying story for use in a single period, or as a change from a more ambitious undertaking. Discussion brings out the moral, which children of eight-to-ten comprehend easily.

The Sun and the Wind and *The Country Mouse and the City Mouse* are favorites with many children. They also provide excellent opportunities for pantomime, as well as ideas for discussion. A group of fables, incidentally, makes a good program without taxing either teacher or players.

A story that appeals to both boys and girls, and is easy to play in a small area, is the tale of *Darby and Joan*. There are only three characters but the story is so short that, unless a group is large, every boy and girl may have a chance to try one of the parts.

DARBY AND JOAN

Have you ever seen a little house about the size of a birdhouse, with two doors in front marked "Fair" and "Rain"? And have you ever noticed that a little woman stands in the doorway marked "Fair," and a little man in the doorway marked "Rain"? And, depending on the weather, that one is always out while the other is in? Well, this little man and woman are known as Darby and Joan, and the following story is told of how they came to be there.

Many years ago Darby and Joan lived happily in a little cottage together. As time went on, however, they began to quarrel. Regardless of how peaceably the day had begun, before long they were disagreeing and finding fault with one another. And so a spell was put on them: from that day forth, one must be out while the other was in, depending on the weather. Our story begins many years later. The day has been fair but the weather is beginning to change, and Darby is about to come out, allowing Joan to go inside and finish her housework. As they talk together, not seeing each other, they regret the quarreling that led to their punishment.

"How I wish I could see you, Joan. Do you realize it has been ten years since we sat down at the table together?"

"I know, Darby. I'm sure if we could be released from this spell, we should never quarrel again."

"Imagine not seeing one's own wife for ten years. It was too cruel a punishment."

As they are talking together, Darby notices someone approaching the cottage. He calls out, "It's beginning to rain. Won't you stop and rest here for a bit?"

The stranger, who is a Fairy in disguise, comes to the doorway and asks Darby why it is he is standing out in the rain while his wife stays in the house. He explains, and sighs over their misfortune. The Fairy then tells him who she is, and offers to release them from their spell but only on condition that they never quarrel again. They agree joyfully, and the Fairy goes off, but not without warning them that if they do quarrel, they will be put under the spell again, and this time it will be forever.

The old couple can scarcely believe their good fortune as they move their arms and legs stiffly and venture outside together. The rain is clearing, and they decide to have supper in front of the cottage. Darby brings out the table and chairs while Joan gets the food. Scarcely have they sat down to eat, however, when Darby criticizes the way Joan slices the bread. Joan replies with annoyance that if he objects, he can cut it himself. Furthermore, she notices that he is wearing his hat at the table. Before they know it, they are quarreling furiously.

Suddenly, the Fairy appears. The old people are stricken. They beg the Fairy for one more chance to try getting along, but she replies, "It is too late. You knew the condition and should have thought of the consequences."

Darby and Joan feel the spell coming on, and slowly move back into their old positions. The Fairy disappears with the old couple once more back in their doorways marked "Fair" and "Rain."

Children of all ages enjoy this story, and have a grand time with the quarrel. First, playing the puppet-like figures while under a spell is a good pantomime for the entire group. Release from the spell gives practice in making the transition from a stiff, controlled stance to free movement. After all have tried it in pantomime, they will be ready to add dialogue. *Darby and Joan* is a delightful little story that calls for strong feeling and changes of mood.

THE COBBLER'S HUMP

There are many versions of this old tale but it never fails to hold a group's interest.

There was once a Cobbler who lived and worked in a small village on the edge of a forest. He was a friendly man, well liked by his neighbors and good at his trade, but he had the misfortune of being a humpback. He was cheerful and uncomplaining, however, and toiled each day, often far into the night. One evening he had some shoes to deliver to a customer in a village a distance away. To reach his destination it was necessary for him to cross a part of the forest. Knowing his way, and therefore being unafraid, he set out, though the sun had long since gone down.

Suddenly he heard the sound of small feet approaching. The Cobbler, startled and curious as to who might be in the woods at this hour, hid behind the trunk of a tree. To his astonishment, a band of elves appeared and danced in a clearing near his hiding place. As the moon came up and the Cobbler could see their merry faces, he came out of hiding and made himself known to them. Despite his protests that he could not move as nimbly as they, the elves insisted that he join in their dance. They had a jolly time together, but at length the Cobbler persuaded them that he had to go on, as he had an errand to do before morning. Reluctantly the elves let him go, but not until he had promised to come again the following night. Then, in order to ensure his return, the leader of the band snatched the hump from his back, thinking it to be a prized possession. Amazed and overjoyed, the little Cobbler went his way —running swiftly now, for his burden was gone.

The next morning, when he told his neighbors the story, they could scarcely believe it, but the hump was certainly gone, and they rejoiced with him in his good fortune. Only one among them was envious. This was a greedy Tailor, who wondered why the Cobbler had had such luck. Perhaps he could think of a way to improve his own lot, if he were to have a similar encounter. So, saying nothing to anyone, he decided to set out that evening just as the sun went down. He arrived at the edge of the woods and hid behind a tree, just as the Cobbler said he had done. Before long, the elves appeared, and, as usual, began to dance in the moonlight. Thinking that perhaps he should be rewarded with gold, the Tailor stepped forward boldly and joined in their dance. The elves could not see his face clearly in the moonlight, and so mistook him for the Cobbler. Pleased that their friend had kept his promise, the leader of the band brought forth the hump and placed it squarely on the Tailor's shoulders. The Tailor, not expecting this turn of events, let out a howl of anger. The elves realized their mistake but saw the trick the Tailor had tried to play on them. The Tailor ran back to the village, but for the rest of his life he had to bear the burden from which the kindly old Cobbler had been freed.

After the children have decided what characters are necessary to the telling and what additional ones may be added, they will be ready to determine the scenes. If playing in a large room, one end can be the forest, and the other, the village. If the space is small, the scenes can easily follow in sequence. In order to involve the entire group, it may be wise to begin with the elves. Music will suggest dance movement, from which the scene will naturally develop. This may be followed by the group, all playing the Cobbler: how he moves, walks, sits, dances, and runs. When the group has become thoroughly involved in the action, they will want to move on to the enactment of scenes. Again, allowing small groups to play bits of the story, each will have an opportunity to contribute dialogue, characterization, and movement. Some groups can be villagers, creating individual characters and showing their attitudes toward the Cobbler and the Tailor. An experienced group may provide an earlier scene in which the Tailor reveals his greediness, thus justifying the unfortunate consequence of his plot.

The story may be introduced through music or through a discussion of human qualities, such as greed or envy. Simple as it is, there is opportunity for creative thinking and feeling, as well as physical movement. Like *Caps for Sale,* it will be as simple or as richly detailed as the group is able to make it.

SUMMARY

The preceding stories were selected for inclusion because of their simplicity and successful use with beginning groups of all ages. Though children's stories, each one has been used with both children and adults, and each age brings its own insights, meanings, and humor. There are many excellent stories just as suitable for beginning creative playing, and the interested leader will have no difficulty finding them. Tastes and interests of the group will guide the selection, though one of the values in creative dramatics is the opportunity it offers for introducing new material and good literature. One thing the leader will discover is that no two groups ever handle a story in quite the same way; if he is able to present it without a preconceived plan as to how it should be done, he will find that every group brings original ideas to its playing.

The procedures suggested are essentially the same, regardless of age level:

1. Presentation of the story.
2. Organization of the material.
3. Improvisation.

4. Evaluation.
5. Re-playing.

Evaluation is an important aspect of creative dramatics and leads into the re-playing, which should acquire new depth and richer detail. Changing parts with each playing may not always make for a better performance, but it does give each participant a chance to play the part of his choice at least once. When the leader feels that the group has gone as far as it can with the story, he may suggest that the group cast it for one final playing. This usually makes for a successful conclusion: the group has created something of its own, and has found the last playing to be the most rewarding.

The older the participants, the more preliminary planning the leader can expect. Children, on the other hand, tend to move quickly into improvisation. Their dialogue will be brief, and the scenes shorter than planned, but their attack is direct. Children, less conditioned to the conventions of the proscenium stage, are likewise freer in their use of space, planning scenes in various parts of the room simultaneously. When the class is held in a room with a stage at one end, they are likely to use it as a particular place—perhaps a mountain top or a distant land—rather than considering it as the central playing area. For every age group there are fewer inhibitions if a large room, instead of a stage, is used. Playing in the round reduces self-consciousness and is conducive to freer movement, since the scattered observers do not seem so much like an audience.

When the group has shown that it can handle the problems of simple fables and stories, it is ready to move on to more demanding material. In the next chapter, longer stories are included, illustrating the possibilities offered for characterization and multiple-scene planning.

CHAPTER 7

Building Plays From Longer Stories

In this chapter, several longer stories are included, with descriptions of some of the ways in which groups have used them. Again, let it be emphasized that there is no right way to dramatize the material. There are as many ways as there are groups, and the illustrations given here merely describe what some groups have done with them. Not only are the plots of these stories more detailed, the characters are complex, and, therefore, require more experience to develop than those in the preceding chapter. The stories have been chosen for the possibilities they offer to the group ready to undertake them.

THE GOLDEN TOUCH

The Golden Touch is a story to which most groups respond. It may be used on various levels because of the theme and lively action. Younger children with some previous experience enjoy the magic, whereas older children find in it a meaning that is pertinent to their own lives. Perhaps a discussion of values will lead most naturally into the telling. The story, on the other hand, may fit into a program that is integrated with literature or social studies. However and wherever it is introduced, *The Golden Touch,* with its rapid and logical sequence of events, makes for good drama. Although the story is familiar, a brief résumé is included before discussing it as material for creative playing.

There was once a very rich king named Midas, who loved nothing in the world so well as his gold, unless it was his little daughter. He even named the child Marigold because her hair shone in the sunlight like the golden coins in the storeroom of his palace. Every morning, after breakfast, he would go down to this storeroom and lock himself in with his treasures. Then he would count all the coins and stand them up in neat piles. He would gaze on his jewels and sigh that he had collected so little. He often wished for another lifetime in which to amass more treasures. There was a time earlier in his life when he had loved music and flowers. Now, however, he preferred the gold in his chests to the petals of roses, and the clink of his coins to any other sound.

One morning, while he was in the storeroom counting his treasures, he saw a shadow fall across the room. He knew he had locked the door carefully and that no one could enter through the small window that let in the one shaft of light. Frightened, he looked up and beheld a tall stranger standing before him. The stranger's face was pleasant, and he smiled as he spoke. Somehow, Midas knew that this was no ordinary mortal. "You are very rich, King Midas," remarked the stranger. Midas shrugged and replied that this was indeed true but that he was dissatisfied.

"Why," said the stranger, "what more could you wish?"

"I should like to have everything I touch turn into gold."

"The golden touch," nodded the stranger. "Are you sure that would please you?"

King Midas was quite sure that it would, so the stranger promised to help him. He told the king that the next morning he could expect the golden touch to come with the sunrise. With that, he vanished as suddenly as he had appeared.

King Midas could scarcely wait for the dawn. He was awake with the first rays of the sun and eagerly reached out to touch his bed covers. At once the soft coverlet became cold and hard with threads of pure gold. Midas leapt out of bed and ran from one object to another, exclaiming in delight as they turned to gold at his touch. To be sure, his clothes were heavy and stiff, but he dismissed this discomfort as a minor disadvantage of his new power. Presently he went out into the garden, where every rose he touched turned at once into gold. Even the grass under his feet turned from green to gold as he walked. So much unaccustomed exercise and such great excitement gave him an appetite, and he soon returned to the palace for breakfast.

Just as he sat down at the table, his little daughter Marigold came into the room, sobbing as she laid an armful of the stiff golden roses on the chair beside her. Midas was distressed at her tears, for normally she had the sunniest disposition in the world. He tried to comfort her, telling her that the golden roses were far more valuable than ordinary flowers, which soon wither and die. Obediently Marigold dried her tears and tried to eat the breakfast that was set before her.

Eagerly, then, her father reached for some fruit, but no sooner had he touched it than it turned into gold. Next he picked up his goblet, but it became gold before he could get it to his lips as did the water in it. Poor Midas cried out in distress, for he had not counted on this. Hearing his cry, Marigold slipped from her chair and ran to her father's side. The king put his arms about the child's waist without a thought as to the consequences. At once her soft little body became as still and hard as a statue, as it, too, turned into the brightest of gold. Horrified at the results of his foolish wish, Midas called out in anguish.

Suddenly the long shadow once again fell across the room and the tall stranger, who had appeared the previous day, stood before him.

"Take it away," begged Midas. "Please take it away."

"You mean you don't want the golden touch, after all?" asked the stranger.

"No," replied Midas. "It is hateful. Take it away."

The stranger considered his request. "It will be more difficult to remove than acquire." Finally, however, he described the one way the golden touch could be lost. The king must go to the brook and bathe in its water. Then he must fill a pitcher and pour the water over everything he wished restored to its natural state.

Midas lost no time in carrying out the stranger's directions. He plunged into the brook and, miraculously, the heavy golden garments lost their weight as they changed back into velvet. He sprinkled some of the water on the nearest flowers, and at once they turned soft and fragrant again. Then he ran back to the palace dining room and poured the rest of the contents on his daughter. At once she moved, and began to brush the water from her hair and frock. Midas was overjoyed to see her living and breathing once more, and clasped her to his heart.

Though, afterward, she often asked him what had happened, Midas never told her what had taken place as a result of his greed; but from that day forth, he lost his interest in gold. The bright yellow glint in his daughter's hair was enough to remind him, should he ever forget, what had so nearly cost him his life and his greatest treasure.

There are many more detailed versions of this story, and it would be wise for the leader to select the one that pleases him most. This synopsis is sufficient, however, to suggest some procedures that might be followed in playing it.

Three characters are obviously needed, but there are opportunities for additional roles, if desired, and a group is usually quick to see them. Servants come to mind first, and are, in fact, of real value in handling the necessary exposition. In planning the scenes, children often suggest many more than will ultimately be needed. The leader will find that as the plans for dramatizing the story take shape, the children see ways in which to compress the action and so reduce the number of characters. Whether the story is finally played in three, four, five, or six different scenes, however, there is little difficulty encountered, for the action builds directly to a strong climax and logical denouement.

Some groups see the story as beginning in the storeroom with Midas counting his treasures. One group created a preliminary scene, in which a nobleman presented the king with a gift, thereby using dramatic action to reveal the character. Another group showed Midas first in his garden at an earlier period in his life, enjoying his flowers and listening to the songs of birds. Still another used a narrator to set the stage and introduce the scenes. The thinking that is done while planning the improvisation is always a valuable aspect of the session. The more carefully this is done, the more rewarding will be the results. Again, it is wise to work on one small scene at a time rather than to attempt to play the whole story. Discussion and evaluation after the playing enable the group to invest the plot with details, and to see each character in greater depth. The first attempts are apt to be thin, in spite of the most thoughtful planning, but a second, third, fourth, or fifth playing, under encouraging guidance, will usually help the group bring *The Golden Touch* to a satisfying level.

Because there are relatively few characters in this story, it is wise to change actors with each new playing of a scene. Much more dialogue is required of the three principals than was true of the stories in the last chapter, and there are no large groups like the villagers and monkeys to occupy the other members of the class. By changing the cast frequently, however, all children can play at one time or another. For most groups, this is a satisfactory method. Their attention is held because they know that they will soon have an opportunity for active participation.

A good group pantomime, which can precede the improvisation, is having everyone move about the room as if suddenly able to turn various objects into gold. Practice with the golden touch is good exercise, and fun for everyone. Ten minutes or so of this bit of pantomime will suffice to involve the group thoroughly, and thus help them get into the story. Again, let it be repeated that the suggestions made here represent only some of the ways in which this story can be introduced and handled. The age, experience, and size of the group will determine procedures, whereas the length and frequency of the class sessions will affect the amount that can be accomplished at one time. Younger and less experienced children cannot be expected to create the richness of detail that an older group will be capable of giving the story. Neither will they, nor should they, be expected to evaluate results. Although the evaluation period provides an excellent opportunity to develop critical thinking in older children, it should never be labored or stressed to the point that the fun of creating is sacrificed.

THE STONE IN THE ROAD

A story that is a particular favorite of many groups is *The Stone in the Road*. The basic idea, the simple plot, and the opportunity of adding characters without destroying or distorting the story make it excellent material for improvisation. For these reasons it has been selected for discussion here. The story is perhaps less well known than the preceding ones, but it is available, and if the leader wishes a more detailed version, he should have no difficulty in obtaining it. Briefly, however, it is told as follows:

> There was once a very rich Duke who took pride in his estate and excellent care of his people. Indeed, no one could be found

with a kinder heart or greater willingness to improve the lot of others. He not only shared his wealth but personally aided all those who came to him with their troubles. Whether it was a new barn, money for a cow, or sickness in a family, the Duke could be counted on for assistance. As the years went by, however, it became apparent that so much help had not strengthened the people. More and more, they depended on their benefactor rather than solving their problems themselves. Nor would they help a neighbor in distress. They simply referred the matter to the Duke, or—worse yet—blamed him for anything that went amiss anywhere in the country.

This troubled the Duke. He began to wonder whether there was anyone in the whole countryside who would make an effort to help himself, let alone another. He thought and thought about it, and finally determined to find out for himself if such a person existed. Very early one morning, he and his servant left the castle and started down the road toward the village. When they reached a particular bend in the highway, the Duke stopped. "Let us move this stone into the middle of the road," he said.

The two men pushed and tugged and worked at it. Finally, with all the strength they could muster, they succeeded in moving the great rock into the middle of the highway. Next, the Duke pulled a small bag from his pocket and carefully tucked it out of sight under the stone. Then he asked his servant to come with him to a spot behind some bushes where they had a good view of the road without being seen. Scarcely had they settled themselves when the first of a long procession approached. It was a farmer on his way to market. Seeing the great stone, he stopped and complained bitterly of the inconvenience it caused him. Though he and his son had great difficulty finding a place wide enough for their sheep to pass by, it never occurred to either of them to remove the obstacle.

Next came two young girls on their way to market. Indeed, they even sat down on the stone to rest for a bit, and talked over what they might buy with the money they hoped to make from the sale of their eggs and flowers. Presently, they, too, went on. All day, one after another passed down the road: a scholar, a musician, a fine gentleman and his lady, and others. But none offered to move the stone. If they noticed it at all, they only complained that the Duke should take better care of the highway.

The old man's heart was heavy as evening approached. Was there no one who would trouble to move it? Finally, as he was about to go home, he saw a young lad coming around the bend, whistling merrily, with a sack of flour slung over his shoulder. No sooner had he reached the spot than he stopped and put down his burden. "What is that stone doing in the middle of the road?" he said to himself. "Why, someone might fall over it."

With that, he pushed and pulled and tugged, and finally succeeded in moving it to one side. "There," he said, "now people can get past it."

As he turned to pick up his sack of flour, he noticed the small bag the Duke had placed on the ground under the stone. "What can this be?" he said aloud. And finding it filled with gold pieces, added, "I must find the owner."

Overjoyed that someone had taken the trouble to move the stone, the Duke came out of his hiding place and stood before him. "Read what it says," he commanded.

The miller's boy read the words that were tied to it: "This gold is for him who moves the stone."

"It is for you," said the Duke. "At last I have found one person who took the trouble to help his neighbors."

"It was nothing," replied the boy. "But thank you, sir. Thank you."

With that, he ran home swiftly to tell his father and mother all about his adventure, and show them his fortune.

Some groups, particularly younger ones, will be content to play the story exactly as it is told here. Most groups, however, have added scenes for exposition and further character delineation. One group began with a scene in a council room, where several people were awaiting turns, asking for favors. Another group had the Duke take a walking tour of the neighborhood, during which he met up with various lazy or discontented villagers. Another group had the Duke and his wife discuss the situation over their dinner. Another made the servant his confidante, and had them plot in a scene together. Still another created a clever servant who pointed out how the people were taking advantage of his master's generosity, and suggested tricks to find out who, if any, was honest and responsible. More than one group thought there should be an additional scene at the end, showing the miller's boy going home where he proudly presents his fortune. It is a story that may be played in one scene, or several, depending upon the ideas offered by the group.

However it is handled, the theme of the story is clear and strong. With a very large class, many additional characters can be added to the scene on the road. Although the Duke and the miller's boy generally start out being favorites, excellent characterizations of the villagers are possible, and often become desired roles. Before attempting to play it at all, however, pantomimic action of moving the stone, sitting on the stone, and getting around the stone helps the group get into the spirit. The stone may be imaginary, or it may be any large prop that is handy, such as a box or a chair. By the time the group has invested it with size and weight, it has become a stone.

Like the other stories, it will be done differently by every group that attempts it. It has an appeal for a wide range of ages, and children will find in it, and do with it, what they can on their level. Older children will find it good material for discussion, and often want to spend considerable time on it. Younger children will enjoy it for the suspense it offers, and can easily play it with the road running around the room, and no break in the action.

PROMETHEUS

Greek mythology is a rich and generally untapped source of material that can be successfully dramatized. One myth, which has been used many times with success, is the story of Prometheus, who stole fire from the gods. Basic human emotions, and a dramatic story, make it particularly appealing to children from seven to twelve. The idea of a formless earth stirs their imagination and provides an unusual opportunity for creativity. The story must be told carefully, and in considerable detail, since not all children will be familiar with it. Although Greek myths are readily available, a brief synopsis of Prometheus is given here, with suggestions as to ways in which the leader may handle it.

> The Greek gods and goddesses were believed to have dwelt on Mount Olympus, high above the earth. Ruling over them was the

mighty Zeus. Among the young gods, most in favor with Zeus for his bravery in helping defeat the Titans, was Prometheus. One day Zeus and Athena, Goddess of Wisdom, were walking in the garden. They caught sight of Prometheus in the distance, looking down toward the earth. Zeus called to him and asked him what interested him, for he had often seen the young god staring down at the forests and mountains below.

Prometheus replied that he was troubled because the earth was so empty and silent, with no man moving about on its surface. Zeus smiled, and said that for some time he had been considering a reward for the young god. "Prometheus," he suggested, "perhaps you would like to descend to the earth and fashion men out of soil." Prometheus was overjoyed.

"You are wise and kind," added Athena. "When you create man, remember to give him a strong body, a keen mind, and a tender heart. Let him also see that there is a need for beauty as well as for the necessities of life."

"You may give man any gifts you wish except the gift of fire," continued Zeus. "That alone belongs to the gods and must remain on Olympus. When you have fashioned your men and are satisfied with your work, I will come down to earth and blow the breath of life into their bodies."

Prometheus was eager to begin, and went off swiftly. Working with power and skill, he modeled his first man upright and powerful, and called him "Man, the Builder." Then he took more soil and made a second man, who was likewise tall and strong. Putting a few grains of corn in his hand, he named him "Man, the Sower and Reaper." The third man he pronounced "Man, the Hunter," and to him he gave a stone. The fourth he called "Man, the Musician." Finally, he finished his fifth man and proclaimed him "Man, the Thinker."

Scarcely had he stepped back to admire his efforts when the deep voice of Zeus was heard from Olympus. "We are pleased with your men, Prometheus. I shall now come down to blow life into them."

Miraculously, each statue came to life and breathed, and moved, and walked. As the days passed, Prometheus cared for his men and worked with them, teaching them to do the special jobs for which they had been created. The men learned quickly and worked happily. One day, however, the seasons changed. The warm air was replaced by cold winds and snowy weather. The men were cold, and Prometheus was deeply disturbed as he watched them huddling together, trying to keep warm. Finally, he could bear it no longer. He knew he must give them fire.

When he called to Athena for help, she asked, "Do you care so much about your men, Prometheus?"

Prometheus declared that he did.

"Enough to risk the wrath of Zeus?" continued Athena. "He will surely punish you. The one thing he has forbidden them is fire."

"I have made my men, and I must help them, even though I suffer for it," replied Prometheus.

"Very well, then," said Athena. "I will help you find the fire to give them."

As swiftly as he had gone down to earth, Prometheus returned to Olympus to get the fire that he was determined his men must have. Then he called the five together and told them not to be frightened, but to learn to use their new gift. Just as he had taught them other things, he taught them how to use a fire for warmth, and for the cooking of food. He warned them never to let the fire go out. The men were fascinated with the many possibilities of fire, and were soon warm and comfortable again.

It was not long, however, before Zeus learned what had happened. Angrily he told Prometheus that he had disobeyed and must be punished for his act.

"I am ready to accept my punishment, great Zeus," Prometheus replied, "for I cannot let my men suffer from the wind and cold."

"A gift that has been given cannot be recalled," continued the god. "Men now possess fire, but you must pay the price. I shall have you bound by chains to yonder mountain. There you must remain forever, and serve as an example to those who dare to disobey my laws."

So saying, Zeus sent his messenger, Hephaestus, down to seize Prometheus and put him in chains. The men were grieved when they saw the dreadful thing that had happened to their creator and teacher, but their hearts were filled with gratitude for his great gift to mankind.

The discussion preceding the story can take many directions. It may begin with a consideration of human qualities and feelings. It may, on the other hand, begin with man's occupations, and some pantomime suggesting them. It may begin with an analysis of th characters in the story and their conflicts. Eventually, in whatever way the story is introduced, there must be a focus on the characters, their behavior, and the consequences of Prometheus' act.

As in the other stories, the myth will be broken down into scenes before it is acted. Work in pantomime can easily be done with the whole group, for there is rich opportunity here. Together, the children can do the following actions: build a hut, hunt for food, plant a field, make a musical instrument (drum or pipe) and discover how to play it, suggest the beginning of man's thought process. Each activity gives scope for imaginative pantomime. Music may be helpful in stimulating movement, though it is not necessary. Children love playing the statues who come to life and learn to do the things for which they were intended. One whole period may easily be given over to these pantomime activities.

When the players are ready to begin on the story, they may wish to take turns playing gods and men. If playing in a large room, the children may conceive of one end of it as Olympus and the other as the earth. Or, if there is a platform, they may decide to locate Olympus on a higher level. The plot calls for at least three scenes, though some groups may see it in five or six. More than one group has played it using a simultaneous setting, with Zeus and Athena observing and commenting, while Prometheus works. When this approach is used, the scenes may move back and forth without a break, or scene division.

Prometheus is a story strong enough to hold the interest for three or four class sessions, with constructive discussion preceding and following each playing. If the group enjoys the story, other myths may be introduced, for there are many with fine dramatic action, and values that children comprehend. Like the other stories in this chapter, *Prometheus* gains depth and detail with each new playing. The young god's sense of responsibility and compassion for his men begins to emerge, adding another dimension to the character. The conflict between the law of Zeus, and Prometheus' moral courage as he begins to feel for his men, makes for powerful drama. The final playing can be most rewarding, as theme, story, character, and action are unified. The group that has become really in-

us' dilemma will have had a rich experience. This
ited to an older group, though even seven- and
understand and play a simplified version.

ETS

This Indian legend, telling how the first blue bonnet flowers appeared on the earth, is a story that appeals to children of middle and upper grades. Many Indian legends are excellent for improvisation, but this one has a special appeal since it is the story of a child and her sacrifice.

Yellow Star is a little Indian girl, who lives with her father and mother in a village belonging to the Comanche tribe. As the story begins, the Chief calls his people together. He describes the trouble that has come to their village after many weeks without rain. The long drought has caused the brooks to dry up; vegetation is dying, and animals have left the parched plains in search of food. The people sit quietly in a circle around the campfire as they listen to their leader. Then they beat the drums and dance, praying to the Great Spirit for rain. At first, nothing happens. Then, suddenly, they hear the voice of the Great Spirit far in the distance. They stop, put down the drums, and listen: "You are being punished for your selfishness and greed. You have lived in a land of plenty for many years, but your people have not shared with their brothers."

The Chief begs for mercy, but the Great Spirit replies, "I will forgive your tribe and send you the water you need only when one among you sacrifices on the campfire that which is dearest to his heart."

Excitedly, the braves talk together. They suggest that one give his horse, another his jewelry, and that still another offer his beautiful young squaw to the Great Spirit. No one, however, is willing to make a sacrifice for the sake of his brothers, and so they move from the campfire and start slowly off toward their homes. The Chief calls them. "Come to this place again in the morning. By that time one among you may have found the gift that will bring us all forgiveness."

The people slowly disappear, each hoping that someone will think of a way to save them. Only little Yellow Star remains. In her arms she carries her fawn-skin doll with its bonnet of blue jay feathers. The doll is her dearest possession. She realizes that she must throw it into the fire to please the Great Spirit, but it is not easy to part with her only toy. Finally, she reaches her decision, as night falls on the village, and she tells the Great Spirit that she is ready to give that which is dearest to her heart. She watches the doll burn slowly, then, seeing the blue feather bonnet lying in the ashes, she picks it up and throws it into the flames. To her amazement, the feathers do not burn, but become small blue flowers. Yellow Star knows, then, that the Great Spirit has accepted her gift, and with a light heart she runs home.

The next morning, all of the Indians gather together as their Chief has commanded, but where only last night there was a campfire, there is now a huge bed of blue flowers. The people are mystified, for they cannot understand how flowers could have sprung up in the hard, dry earth.

Yellow Star's mother tells the Chief about the doll. "Surely," she says, "it must be a sign. Hundreds of flowers now grow on ground that was trampled and dry."

The people, however, are unwilling to believe her story, for why should the Great Spirit be satisfied with so small a gift as a child's fawn-skin doll? At that moment, there is a roll of thunder in the distance. The Chief knows now that the Great Spirit has accepted Yellow Star's offering. Again, he asks his people to beat their drums and give thanks that they have at last been forgiven. The first raindrops fall.

This charming legend gives an opportunity for total group participation. Since movement is an important element, a good beginning can be made with a dance around the campfire. The use of a drum aids enormously in building rhythms, as the Indians move and dance and pray. The leader can, of course, begin with the story, but before dialogue is attempted, practice in rhythmic movement helps the players to become involved.

Discussion of the story and its theme should precede the playing, inasmuch as this will deepen the understanding of a people different in custom, yet like us in their human strengths and weaknesses. When the group is ready to begin, it is again suggested that short scenes, rather than the whole story, be played first. For example, the opening scene, in which the Chief calls his people together and explains the seriousness of their situation, is quite enough for one sequence. Yellow Star's sacrifice is another. The players may conceive of the story as taking place in one act, with a break to indicate passage of time, or they may see it as a play in two or three scenes. Because it is a story in which any number may participate, playing it in the round is desirable, if possible. Players and observers are one, and are, therefore, involved to an unusual degree.

The part of Yellow Star is a favorite, but the Chief, the mother, and the selflsh braves and squaws can all be built into characters who are believable and interesting. If this story finds favor, the leader may wish to bring other Indian legends to class. Most of them require little more than space for playing, since they are concerned with human beings in conflict with nature, and human weaknesses familiar to all.

A LEGEND OF SPRING

Another Indian legend, which has proved extremely successful for creative playing, is *A Legend of Spring.* It is simple in plot but provides a wonderful opportunity for group pantomime and movement. Players of all ages find it appealing, and develop it in proportion to their experience and the time that is given them.

The Indians of the great plains had suffered through a long winter, but this year no sign of spring had appeared. Neither sun nor wind nor warm rains had come to awaken the seeds or bring the wild animals out of their winter hiding. One day, the Chief of the tribe called all the braves and squaws together. He explained to them that unless food were found soon, they would have to abandon their village and seek a home elsewhere. There was silence. The people looked up at the cold, gray sky, and down at the hard frozen earth. They knew the Chief was right, yet no one wanted to leave the pleasant valley in which they had dwelt for so many years. Finally White Cloud, youngest and strongest of the braves, spoke out. "I will go into the forest in search of food. With my strong bow and arrows, surely I can find food to bring back to my people."

"I will go with you," cried a second, then a third and a fourth.

Others rose from the campfire, where they had been sitting, and joined him. The old Chief smiled. "Go," he said. "Perhaps if you hunt deep enough in the forest you will find the deer and rabbits to provide food until the spring comes to our land. While you are absent, we shall pray to the Great Spirit to make the sun shine again and the clouds empty warm rain on our fields."

The young men ran out as the drums beat a farewell. Then the old Chief called to the Great Spirit for help. The people danced around the fire, asking for sun, rain, and wind for their planting, and game for their hunters. When they finally dropped to their knees, exhausted, there was a rustle in the bushes. Looking up, they beheld a large golden bird flying toward the clearing. Scarcely had it appeared when White Cloud and his band of hunters broke through the underbrush. Two or three of the men had already raised their bows when White Cloud spoke.

"Do not shoot the golden bird. Perhaps it has come from the Great Spirit. It may be a sign for us if we wait to see what it wants. Hold your arrows. Do not shoot!"

The braves put down their bows and waited. Then the golden bird, seeing that the people meant her no harm, glided gracefully into their midst. Suddenly, she was transformed into a lovely young maiden with a golden bow and arrow.

"I have come from the Great Spirit," she said. "Listen to me carefully. Here is an arrow which one of you must shoot straight into the dark cloud overhead. If the cloud is pierced, the rains will begin, and winter will leave your valley. If he who shoots the arrow does not succeed, you must prepare to leave your homes, for spring will not come this year."

So saying, she handed the bow to the Chief, asking him to select the brave who could shoot the straightest arrow. "You choose, golden maiden," he said. "It is your arrow. You choose the one who will send it from the bow."

Slowly the maiden circled the campfire, first looking at one, then another. Finally she stopped before White Cloud and handed him the golden bow and arrow. He took it from her silently, aimed at the cloud and released it. Up and up it went until it was lost from sight. Then, suddenly, a crack appeared in the sky. The sun came out and the warm spring rain began to fall. The drum beat joyously as the people danced again, this time in thanks to the Great Spirit, who had answered their prayers.

Like the other Indian legend, this one is best begun with movement. Pantomime and dance, expressing the people's need for rain, wind, and sun, help the group get into the story. Hunting, fishing, planting, eating, and moving camp are activities that may also be expressed in pantomime by each member of the group. If a sufficiently long time is spent on movement and pantomime, many ideas will come that can later be incorporated into the story. Children love to think of as many ways as possible to show how the Indians lived, and of how they expressed their needs to the Great Spirit. Actually, the whole story can be played without words, although most groups will want to invent some dialogue. A drum is a valuable property for the leader at first, but he will want to pass it along to one of the participants later. Some groups see the story in a single scene; others may wish to break it into several. However it is handled, *A Legend of Spring* is a strong story for creative playing. A drum and plenty of space in which to move freely are the only requirements.

SUMMARY

Because of the greater plot complications and length, all of these stories will demand more time in planning than those in the preceding chapter. There is sufficient content to absorb the interest of the average group for several sessions, depending, of course, on the length of the class periods and the age of the participants. Characters are presented in greater depth, hence much more time must be spent on their development. Most groups like to consider such questions as:

1. What is the character really like?
2. Why does he behave as he does?
3. What do others think of him? Why?
4. If he is not like that, why do they think so?
5. How is he changed, or what has he learned as a result of his actions?

As the participants grow in experience, they will find new ways of telling the story. Some will want to use narrators; others, many scenes; and some may rearrange the sequence of events altogether. As was said in the previous chapter, every group is unique, and the leader learns to expect an endless variety of ways in which the same material can be handled and interpreted. The growing self-confidence of the players releases ideas, which lead to further thinking and experimentation. Each group, regardless of age, becomes more critical of its efforts as, with the help of the leader, it strives for a higher level of accomplishment.

CHAPTER 8

The Possibilities in Poetry

Children like poetry. They are sensitive to the rhythm of it, and enjoy the repetition of sounds, words, and phrases. The direct approach of the poet is not unlike their own; hence poetry, unless it has been spoiled for them, has a special appeal. The music and language, as well as the ideas, feelings, and images of poetry reach the younger child particularly, capturing and stimulating his imagination. For this reason, poetry can be used in creative dramatics, often with highly successful results.

Many leaders find poetry a more satisfactory springboard than prose for introducing creative playing to a group. This is probably an individual matter, depending as much on the leader as the participants. If the leader, or teacher, enjoys poetry himself, he will find that it provides a rich source of material that can be used at all levels of experience, and with all ages. For children, poetry and play go quite naturally together. "The affinity between poetry and play is not external only; it is also apparent in the structure of creative imagination itself. In the turning of a poetic phrase, the development of a motif, the expression of a mood, there is always a play element at work." [1]

For these reasons, the possibilities in poetry as motivation are considered. What kinds of poems are usable? How can poetry and movement be combined? Has choral speaking any place in creative dramatics? For the answers to these questions, one has only to go to children, themselves, as they engage in their play. Many of their games are accomplished by chants, which are a form of choral speaking. In action games, rhythm is basic, while some games are played to verse with the players often making up their own original

1. L. Huizinga, *op. cit.*, p. 132.

stanzas. If we listen, we note the enjoyment of repetition, refrain, and the sounds of words. It is very much later that poetry becomes a literary form to be taken seriously, and when it does, the element of play is, unfortunately, too often lost.

CHORAL SPEAKING

Because poetry lends itself so well to group enjoyment, let us begin with a consideration of choral speaking, its purposes and procedures. Choral reading, or speaking, is simply reading or reciting in unison under the direction of a leader. It is not a new technique, for people have engaged in it for centuries. It antedated the theatre in the presentation of ideas, and became an important element of the Greek drama. Evidences of choral speaking have been found in the religious ceremonies and festivals of primitive peoples, while today it is still used for ritualistic purposes in church services, and on patriotic occasions. Recently, however, it has been recognized as one of the most effective methods of teaching the language arts and improving speech habits. When working with older children or adults, the two major purposes of the activity are:

1. Learning (when the purpose is process and, therefore, participant-centered).
2. Performance (when the purpose is program and, therefore, audience-centered).

Often the former leads into the latter, but, like creative dramatics, it does not necessarily follow that practice must result in performance. Practice has values of its own, whether or not the product is shared.

Values

One of the values of choral speaking is that it can be used successfully, regardless of space or class size. While a group of twenty or so is more desirable than one of forty or fifty, the larger number need not be a deterrent.

Many teachers consider the greatest value of choral speaking the opportunity it provides for speech improvement. Pitch, volume, rate, and tone quality are important to the effective interpretation of material. The need for clear diction is apparent when a group is reading aloud, whereas the practicing of speech sounds alone is often a tedious and unrelated exercise. During discussion, even young children will make suggestions as to how a poem should be recited. Vocal expression and the clear enunciation of speech sounds are often acquired more easily and with greater motivation when the group works together on meaning.

A third value, and one shared with creative dramatics, is the opportunity it provides for social cooperation. Choral speaking is a group activity, and by its nature, therefore, directs each individual to a common goal. The child with the strident voice learns to soften his tone, whereas the shy child can work for more volume without feeling self-conscious. Even the speech-handicapped may recite without embarrassment because he is not speaking alone, and, therefore, is not conspicuous.

A fourth value of choral speaking is its suitability to any age level. It may be introduced in the kindergarten but is equally effective when used in high school or college classes. Not all material is adapted to choral work, but much of it is, and the major criterion is probably that it be enjoyed and recommended by the readers themselves.

Procedures

There are many ways of beginning choral speaking, but with younger children, it will probably spring from their own enjoyment of a poem, and their obvious desire to say it aloud or to the accompaniment of action. With older children, who have had no experience in group reading, the teacher will not only select the material with care but will give some thought in advance to its interpretation. Discussion of the meaning, and the various ways of reading it so as to bring out the meaning, gives the pupils a part in planning it. A second reading will reveal further meaning, as well as difficulties in phrasing and diction.

As the group becomes more experienced, it will offer suggestions as to those lines that may be most effectively taken by the whole group, part of the group, and by individual voices. Although a structured activity, choral speaking offers a real opportunity for creative thinking, as each group works out its own presentation. The teacher leads, indicating when to start, and watches the phrasing, emphases, and pauses suggested by the readers. The amount of time spent on a poem will vary, but it is more important to keep the enthusiasm alive than it is to work for perfection. With practice, the group will grow increasingly sensitive to the demands of different kinds of material, and their results will improve in proportion to their understanding and enjoyment.

Most authorities on choral speaking suggest dividing the group into light and dark voices. This is not quite the same as a division into high and low, or soprano and alto voices, but has to do with quality and resonance as well as pitch. Some leaders, on the other hand, believe that a division in which there are both light and dark in each group makes for more interesting quality. However it is done, some division is necessary for any group of more than ten variation. Some poems, particularly short ones, are most effective if the class is very large. These may be the middle voices; though, again, it is the material that will suggest the groupings rather than an arbitrary division.

Ways of Reading

Unison—The whole group reads together. Though the simplest in one sense, this is the most difficult, since using all voices limits variation. Some poems, particularly short ones, are most effective when read or spoken by the entire class.

Antiphonal—This is a division into two groups with each taking certain parts. Many poems are more effective when read in this way. The poem will dictate the way it may be read.

Cumulative—When this technique is used, it is for the purpose of building toward a climax, or certain high points in the poem. As the term suggests, it is the accumulation of voices, either individually, or by groups.

Solo—Often lines or stanzas call for individual reading. This can be an effective technique as well as a way of giving an opportunity for individual participation.

Line-around—This is solo work, in which each line is taken by a different reader. Children enjoy this, and are alert to the lines they have been assigned.

As the group progresses, and attempts longer and more difficult material, it may suggest using several or all of these techniques in one poem. The results can be remarkably effective, encouraging attentiveness and self-discipline as well as imaginative planning. Occasionally, sound effects can be added. Music, bells, drums, and vocal sounds, produced by the readers themselves, provide an opportunity for further inventiveness.

Because our primary concern is creative dramatics, only those poems that suggest movement or pantomime are included here. The following have been used successfully with groups, combining choral speaking and activities suggested by the content or sounds. The first, *Happy New Year,* is an old rhyme, suggesting the simplest kind of movement as a beginning:

Happy New Year! Happy New Year!
I've come to wish you a Happy New Year.
I've got a little pocket and it is very thin.
Please give me a penny to put some money in.
If you haven't got a penny, a halfpenny will do.
If you haven't got a halfpenny, well—
God bless you!

In England, children went caroling from house to house on New Year's Day. Their neighbors gave them money, much as we give candy and apples for Trick-or-Treat on Hallowe'en. Whether they received a contribution or not, they sang or spoke, and this old rhyme has been handed down. The group can say the verse together, with one child acting the part of the caroler; or half of the group can speak, with the other half playing the carolers. Perhaps the entire group will want to speak and move. There are various possibilities in even as short a rhyme as this.

A very simple verse, but one that offers an unusual opportunity for imaginative movement, is *Jump or Jiggle.* Not only children, but adult students get into the spirit of it, and have a good time thinking of movements that characterize the animals mentioned.

JUMP OR JIGGLE

Evelyn Beyer

Frogs jump.
Caterpillars hump.
Worms wiggle.
Bugs jiggle.
Rabbits hop.
Horses clop.
Snakes slide.
Sea gulls glide.
Mice creep.
Deer leap.
Puppies bounce.
Lions stalk—
But
I walk.

The next verse suggests the use of sound effects rather than action. Part of the group might say the first and third lines, with the others taking the second and fourth. Or, if two clocks are suggested, a solo voice might take the first and third, with the total group taking the other lines. Even so simple a poem as this provides some opportunity for inventiveness.

Slowly ticks the big clock:
  Tick-tock, tick-tock!
But cuckoo clock ticks a double quick:
  Tick-a-tock-a, tick-a-tock-a,
Tick-a-tock-a, tick!

Gallop Away is one of a number of old ballads that provide excellent material for combining choral speaking and movement.

One way of allocating parts is suggested, but there are many others, and it is a good idea to try several before settling on one.

GALLOP AWAY

LIGHT: Dicky set out for Wisdom Hall,
On Mistress Anne to make a call;

ALL: Gallop away, gallop away,
Gallop away for aye, for aye.

DARK: Dicky put on his Sunday clothes,
Scarlet waistcoat, and white hose;

ALL: Gallop away, gallop away,
Gallop away for aye, for aye.

DARK: Dicky mounted his dapple grey,
Smacked his whip and galloped away;

ALL: Gallop away, gallop away,
Gallop away for aye, for aye.

LIGHT: Mistress Anne came tripping away
To hear what Dicky had got to say;

ALL: Gallop away, gallop away,
Gallop away for aye, for aye.

SOLO 1: In she came with a bow and a smile,
"You haven't been here, Master Dick, for a while."

ALL: Gallop away, gallop away,
Gallop away for aye, for aye.

SOLO 2: "Oh, I've been busy with cutting the corn.
My pigs are killed, and my sheep are shorn."

ALL: Gallop away, gallop away,
Gallop away for aye, for aye.

SOLO 2: "But I have no one to cure my hams,
To spin my wool, to make my jams."

ALL: Gallop away, gallop away,
Gallop away for aye, for aye.

SOLO 2: "So come, Mistress Anne, away with me,
My house to keep, and my wife to be."

ALL: Gallop away, gallop away,
Gallop away for aye, for aye.

LIGHT: Mistress Anne, having household skill,
And loving Dicky, said

SOLO 1: "I will."

ALL: Gallop away, gallop away,
Gallop away for aye, for aye.

Two children can act the story while it is being told. Or, several pairs can act it at the same time if the class is very large. The galloping rhythm appeals to younger children, and the pantomime is so simple it can be done by children of any age. The interest lies in the repetition of sounds, the refrain, and the narrative, which demands little in the way of characterization.

Taffy Was a Welshman is an old rhyme suggesting considerable physical activity. Like many nursery rhymes, it contains violence, but also humor, and children do enjoy it.

TAFFY WAS A WELSHMAN

Taffy was a Welshman, Taffy was a thief;
Taffy came to my house and stole a piece of beef;

I went to Taffy's house, Taffy wasn't home;
Taffy came to my house and stole a marrow-bone.
I went to Taffy's house, Taffy wasn't in.
Taffy came to my house and stole a silver pin;
I went to Taffy's house, Taffy was in bed,
I took up a poker and flung it at his head.

There are various ways in which this rhyme can be handled. The total group might read or recite it while two children act; or, one group might take the first, second, fourth, and sixth lines, while the second group takes the third, fifth, seventh, and eighth. The appeal lies in the repetition and the humor. Children like to pantomime the action, and if the horses are placed at each side of the room, it begins to take on the semblance of a play, with two characters in conflict.

MERRY-GO-ROUND

Dorothy Baruch

I climbed up on the merry-go-round,
And it went round and round.

I climbed up on a big brown horse,
And it went up and down.

Around and round and up and down,
Around and round and up and down.

I sat high up on a big brown horse,
And rode around on the merry-go-round,
And rode around on the merry-go-round.
I rode around on the merry-go-round
Around
And round
And
Round.

This poem is fun for children of all ages because of the action, which requires some coordination. As with the others, half of the group can read it while the other half acts the merry-go-round; or, if the group is small, everyone can do the action while repeating the lines. It is probably more satisfactory handled the first way, with variety achieved by having individual voices take the lines beginning with "I." Sometimes children like to imagine the merry-go-round running down until it comes to a stop.

ECHO

Author Unknown

I sometimes wonder where he lives,
This Echo that I never see.
I heard his voice now in the hedge,
Then down behind the willow tree.

And when I call, "Oh, please come out,"
"Come out," he always quick replies.
"Hello, hello," again I say;
"Hello, hello," he softly cries.

He must be jolly, Echo must,
For when I laugh, "Ho, ho, ho, ho,"
He answers me with "Ho, ho, ho."

I think perhaps he'd like to play;
I know some splendid things to do.
He must be lonely hiding there;
I wouldn't like it. Now, would you?

Echoes are fascinating, and this poem is one that may prompt a group to make up an original story about echoes. It lends itself so well to choral reading that it is suggested the class try it this way first, then discuss whether something else might be done with it. The lines, in which the Echo speaks, are good solo lines that stimulate speculation as to who the Echo is, what he is like, where he is hiding, and whether or not he is ever discovered. Some groups have made up delightful stories about him after reading the poem together first.

Although choral speaking is an effective way to begin pantomime, it is not the only way of using poetry. Often a poem can be introduced by the leader, either before or after improvisation. It may serve as a springboard to action in which the whole class participates but does not necessarily repeat or read the verse. One short poem that has proved highly successful with many groups of all ages is *Hallowe'en.*

HALLOWE'EN

Geraldine Brain Siks

Sh! Hst!
Hssst! Shssssh!
It's Hallowe'en.
Eerie creatures now are seen.
Black, bent witches fly
Like ugly shadows through the sky.
White, stiff ghosts do float
Silently, like mystery smoke.

Lighted pumpkins glow
With crooked eyes and grins to show
It's Hallowe'en.
Hssst! Shssh!
Sh! Hst!

The period might start off with a discussion of what we think of when we hear the word, Hallowe'en. Most groups suggest pumpkins, witches, orange and black, elves, broomsticks, cats, night, ghosts, trick-or-treat, and masks. Some pantomime to music can be introduced here, with the whole class becoming witches, cats, or ghosts. After they are thoroughly in the spirit of Hallowe'en, the poem can be read. When the group is small, all may be eerie creatures, witches, and ghosts. When the group is large, it can be divided into several parts, with each one choosing one idea to pantomime. Pumpkins have been suggested in a variety of ways: rolling about on the floor in rounded shapes, squatting with big smiles, and moving in circles to music. Music is helpful though not necessary. This poem never fails to arouse a response, and on one occasion led to an informal program of Hallowe'en poems and improvisations.

The next poem is one that has been most successful with both children and adults. The universality of its theme appeals to everyone, and stimulates an imaginative response at any time of the year. It was the basis for a delightful improvisation by a group of Puerto Rican teachers, who understood and enjoyed it, then im-improvised it with Spanish dialogue.

SING A SONG OF SEASONS

Alice Ellison

It's spring.
Such a hippity, happity, hoppity
First spring day.
Let's play! Let's play! Let's play!

It's summer!
Such a swingy, swazy, lazy
First hot day.
Let's play! Let's play! Let's play!

It's fall!
Such a brisky, frisky, crispy
First fall day.
Let's play! Let's play! Let's play!

It's winter!
Such a blowy, snowy joy
First winter day.
Let's play! Let's play! Let's play!

Before reading the poem, there can be pantomimes of simple sports and games. Flying kites, skating, tossing a ball, jumping rope, and playing tennis are familiar activities that serve to get the group moving and break down the barriers of self-consciousness. After perhaps fifteen minutes of this kind of activity, the teacher is ready to read the poem. Discussion as to games and sports appropriate to each season directs the thinking, and often brings some unexpected suggestions. After everyone has had a chance to offer ideas, the teacher can ask how the poem might be played.

If the class is separated into four groups, each group can take a season, showing various games and sports belonging to it. Some groups create situations for each, such as going to the beach in summer, with sunbathing, swimming, picnicking, and the like. More than one group has created a scene with characters for each season, using the poem only as a springboard for an original situation. It is urged that this be done in the round, rather than on a stage or in the front of a room, so as to allow for as much movement as possible, and easy passage into the center without breaking the mood.

IMAGININGS

J. Paget-Fredericks

Imagine!
A little red door that leads under a hill
Beneath roots and bright stones and pebbly rill.

Imagine!
A quaint little knocker and shoe scraper, too—
A curious carved key
Is waiting for you.

Imagine!
Tiptoe on doormat, you're turning the key.
The red door would open
And there you'd be.

Imagine!
Shut the door tightly, so no one should see.
And no one would know then
Where you would be.
Imagine, if you can.

A poem such as *Imaginings* lends itself to all kinds of improvisation. Every age will find an answer to the question: what lies behind the little red door? It is a good idea for the teacher to read the poem aloud two or three times before asking what the group sees in it. If the class is not too large, every child may be given a chance to describe what he sees. Younger children find buried treasure, a forbidden city, thieves, a ghost town. Some may describe a place they know, with friends or neighbors inhabiting it. This particular poem is a wonderful springboard for the imagination, since it leads the listener to the threshold, and then leaves him free to follow his own ideas.

Some groups have been stimulated to plan an original play, involving several characters. If many good suggestions come out of the discussion, the leader may want to break the class into small groups of three or four, who will, in turn, dramatize their ideas. Occasionally, if a group is very small, or if the teacher wants to plan an individual lesson, each child may pantomime what he sees and does behind the red door. This poem can hold a group for two or three sessions, depending on their readiness to use the material, and the interest it stimulates.

SOME ONE

Walter de la Mare

Some one came knocking
   At my wee, small door;
Some one came knocking,
   I'm sure—sure—sure;
I listened, I opened,
   I looked to left and right,

But nought there was a-stirring
  In the still dark night;
Only the busy beetle
  Tap-tapping in the wall,
Only from the forest
  The screech owl's call
Only the cricket whistling
  While the dewdrops fall,
So I know not who came knocking
  At all, at all, at all.

Some One has the same power to evoke an imaginative response. Though the poem is short, it creates an atmosphere of mystery and wonder. Who can be knocking? How large is the "wee, small door"? Who am "I"? Do I ever find out who my mysterious visitor was? How do I react? Groups of all ages enjoy imagining this situation, and the teacher may expect a variety of responses and interpretations. Some children have insisted that the door can be no more than a few inches high, which, of course, leads into the question of whose house it is. Fairies, elves, friendly insects, and mice have all been suggested. Other children have seen it as a cottage door—small compared to the doors of city buildings. Visitors, in this case, vary from mysterious strangers with magic powers to actual persons—frightened, and faint with weariness. Indians have been suggested, investigating an early settler's cabin. Because the poet does not say who knocked, the reader is entirely free to create his own situation, and some delightful stories have been inspired as a result.

SEA SHELL

Amy Lowell

Sea Shell, Sea Shell,
  Sing me a song, O please!
A song of ships, and sailor men,
  And parrots, and tropical trees.

Of islands lost in the Spanish Main
Which no man ever may find again,
Of fishes and corals under the waves,
And sea-horses stabled in great green caves.

Sea Shell, Sea Shell,
Sing of the things you know so well.

Although *Sea Shell* offers vivid imagery, it leaves the imagination free to roam tropical isles, and savor adventure. Every child responds to the singing of a shell, and most will go on to ideas of their own. Perhaps having the group tell their own stories is a good beginning. What did you hear? Where did you find the shell? What is it like? What did it sing when you listened? Tell us its story.

Having a collection of shells adds to the interest as the children feel and examine them. Elaborate plays set on unknown shores have resulted, with the boys, in particular, responding to the thoughts of sailors, pirates, and treasures buried in the sand.

WHITE BUTTERFLIES

Algernon Charles Swinburne

Fly, white butterflies, out to sea,
Frail, pale wings for the wind to try,
Small white wings that we scarce can see.
   Fly!

Some fly light as a laugh of glee,
Some fly soft as a long, low sigh:
All to the haven where each would be,
   Fly!

White Butterflies suggests action, and is especially good when used with younger children. Flying involves the whole body, and trying to fly like the various kinds of butterflies is a strong stimulus to different kinds of movement. As many can try it at the same time as space permits, with music as accompaniment. Whereas skipping, galloping, and running are suggested by many poems, the graceful movements of the butterflies provide a quiet change. There are many poems that stimulate action or dance, rather than drama, and these are good to use from time to time for the kinds of responses they elicit.

I HEAR AMERICA SINGING

Walt Whitman

I hear America singing, the varied carols I hear.
Those of mechanics, each one singing his as it should be
 blithe and strong,
The carpenter singing his as he measures his plank or
 beam,
The mason singing his as he makes ready for work, or
 leaves off work.
The boatman singing what belongs to him in his boat,
 the deck-hand singing on the steamboat deck,
The shoemaker singing as he sits on his bench, the hatter
 singing as he stands,
The wood-cutter's song, the ploughboy's on his way in
 the morning, or at noon intermission or at sundown,
The delicious singing of the mother, or of the young wife
 at work, or of the girl sewing or washing.
Each singing what belongs to him or her and to none else.
The day what belongs to the day—at night the party of
 young fellows, robust, friendly.
Singing with open mouths their strong melodious songs.

I Hear America Singing is a grand poem for both choral speaking and dramatization. The various characters and their occupations suggest pantomime to participants of all ages. If playing in a large room, the characters can be scattered about the circle, with any number taking part. Pantomime and speaking may be done simultaneously, or separately, as the group prefers. This is a poem that is particularly appealing to older students, who are often stimulated to further reading of the poet's work. The mood is powerful and usually acts as a unifying element.

SUMMARY

Poetry, in conclusion, is an effective springboard for improvisation. The directness of verse motivates the players to a response that is direct and imaginative. For this reason, it is a good starting point for the beginner, though it can be used at any time with even the most advanced players. Because the sounds of poetry have as great an appeal as the content and mood, it is suggested that poetry be spoken as well as acted.

Choral speaking is a group art and can, therefore, be combined with creative dramatics if the teacher so wishes. Some of the reasons for including choral speaking are as follows:

1. It can be done with groups of any size and age.
2. It emphasizes group rather than individual effort.
3. It provides an opportunity to introduce poetry.
4. It offers the shy or handicapped child an opportunity to speak.
5. It promotes good habits of speech through enjoyable exercise, rather than drill.
6. It is a satisfying activity in itself.
7. It can be combined successfully with rhythmic movement and pantomime.

Just as action songs are used with very young children as an approach to creative rhythms, so may poetry be used with older children, to suggest mood, stimulate ideas, and begin the flow of creative energy. Chants, and the repetition of words, have a natural appeal. Thus poetry and nonsense verse may prove a successful method of introducing creative drama. Skill in movement, rhythms, and pantomime are increased as all children are given opportunities to participate.

CHAPTER 9

A Play for an Audience

Formal dramatics, in contrast to creative dramatics, is primarily audience-centered and has, from the beginning, public performance as its goal. A script is selected in advance, and memorized by the players. It does not matter whether the lines were written by a playwright or the teacher, or composed by the children themselves. The use of a script distinguishes formal dramatics from creative dramatics, and supplies the structure—plot, theme, characters, dialogue—that will be followed.

It would be unwise to attempt to cover both informal and formal dramatic techniques in one book, whatever its length. It is hoped that teachers of young children will confine their efforts to creative dramatics exclusively. But for teachers of older children, a few elementary suggestions are offered as to the smoothest way of moving the play to the stage.

This transition should come easily and naturally to the group that has spent many hours in improvisation. For boys and girls who have played together informally over a period of time, the result is more likely to be one of "sharing" than "showing," and to this end the teacher should be able to help the players achieve their goal—successful communication with an audience. Public performances, regardless of their popularity, should be infrequent, however, and then planned only for other classes or parents. This chapter has been included to help the teacher move, if she must, from informal classroom dramatics to the sharing of an experience with others.

Unless the teacher has had some theatre training, directing the formal play can be a traumatic experience. That is the reason for emphasizing simplicity: a long script, requiring elaborate scenery and costumes, poses problems for the most seasoned director. The average teacher does not have the background, time, or facilities to cope with such problems, but he can support and help enthusiastic young players prepare and demonstrate their work. In guiding beginners of any age, the most important single element is the approach of the leader. His enthusiasm and creative guidance help young players to cross the bridge between self-expression and successful communication.

Creativity is less dependent upon training and past experience than it is upon a special way of feeling, thinking, and responding. It is, therefore, quite possible for the teacher to be a highly creative person without having specialized in the theatre arts. Nevertheless, the formal play does make technical demands, which the teacher must realize; an audience is involved, and, therefore, a product. He must be prepared to take an additional step, by supplying showmanship.

CHOOSING THE SCRIPT

It is to be hoped that the play presented by children in the middle or upper grades will be one they have written themselves. When the script comes as the result of enthusiasm over a good story, or the culmination of their study of a subject, it is much more likely to have meaning for the class. If, for example, a class has been studying another culture (the American Indian, China, the Middle Ages), and they dramatize material relating to it, the play emerges from the background as a natural expression. They may decide they want to dramatize one of the stories or legends they have read. After playing it creatively a number of times, they will be ready to write, or have the teacher write, the dialogue as they suggest it. The results will be childlike and crude, but the story, itself, has stood the test of time and, therefore, serves as a good scenario.

Sometimes a group wants to try an original plot. This is infinitely more difficult. Again, if it comes as the result of great interest in a subject they have been studying, they will know something of the background (time, place, occupations of the people, beliefs, superstitions, education, food, housing, folk or tribal customs). Their very enthusiasm is the primary requisite. Beyond that, they will need the guidance of the teacher in planning a story and developing characters who motivate the action. Inexperienced playwrights of any age cannot be expected to turn out well-made plays. What they *can* do, however, is demonstrate their understanding of the subject matter about which they are writing, and show believable characters involved in the story. The play that comes as the result of integrating drama with social studies, music, literature, dance, or art will have its greatest value to the players. Another class will enjoy seeing their work, and perhaps be stimulated to try a play of its own. These are sufficient reasons for deciding to share the project, but unless the children are older, and the teacher has had considerable experience in dramatics, it should probably not go beyond the school assembly audience.

Occasionally, however, a class will want to do a play that is not related to class work. When this request comes, the problem is somewhat different. There is the question of a good script that will offer as many opportunities as possible, without featuring three or four talented players. There is a scarcity of such material, though there are some good short plays available which have been written with the class, or camp group, specifically in mind. The values cited in an earlier chapter should be considered when making the decision. Is it worthwhile material? Are the characters believable? Does the dialogue offer enrichment? Is the play interesting to the players? Beyond that, we must ask if it has enough parts to involve the whole group in some way.

Often a play written expressly for classroom use will have several major characters, and groups of townsfolk, or a chorus. This gives everyone a chance, makes double casting possible, and may even offer an opportunity to add music or dance. Production problems are another consideration. What are the stage facilities? Or will the play be performed in the classroom? If so, will it be in the round, or proscenium style? Are scenery and costumes essential, or can the script be simply performed with the tables and chairs that are available?

Sometimes the teacher will find a play based on a favorite story. Other times, the children will want to work on a particular kind of play—for example, a mystery. Whatever the choice, it should be a short script, requiring as little time as possible for rehearsals; long periods spent in rehearsing difficult scenes rarely make for a lively experience. If the group does a play for an audience, the choice of a script is the first important consideration.

THE DIRECTOR

The teacher acts as director during the rehearsal periods. Some directors are permissive, and allow much opportunity for individual interpretation. Others plan action carefully in advance and supervise every detail. The director of inexperienced casts often finds his greatest success in an approach that is somewhere between the two extremes: he gives enough direction to make the cast feel secure, but provides enough leeway for individual interpretation and inventiveness. Regardless of method, however, the use of a script and the anticipation of an audience automatically place the emphasis on product rather than process.

Production also implies scenery and costumes; hence time and effort must be given to their design and construction. These need not be elaborate; indeed, they seldom are, in school or camp situations, but the mounting is an important aspect of the formal play. When children can assume some responsibility for scenery, costumes, and properties, additional learning experiences are provided, as well as the opportunity for integrating arts and crafts with dramatics. Cooperation between the players and the backstage crew is essential to success, and is certainly one of the greatest satisfactions a group can experience.

For younger children, however, these values are all too frequently outweighed by anxiety, or boredom, or both, and the results tend to be wooden, lacking freshness and charm. For the child in the middle grades, however, there is occasionally reason for producing a play, provided the script is not too demanding or the direction too rigid. For the older child, on the other hand, the produced play is frequently of great value in teaching dramatic techniques and sharing an art with an audience. For the seventh- or eighth-grader, there are values to be found in the sustained work of production.

Older children delight in the sharing of an activity and enjoy the discipline required to bring the performance to a high level.

It is suggested that before any work on the play is begun, the director have the group play the story creatively. Improvisation helps the players become familiar with the plot, get acquainted with the characters, and remain free in their movement. When the cast is thoroughly acquainted with the story, it is a relatively easy matter to rehearse more formally.

FLOOR PLANS

The director should make a floor plan or diagram of the playing space in advance. On this he will sketch in the essential pieces of scenery, or furniture, and indicate the entrances. This is not a

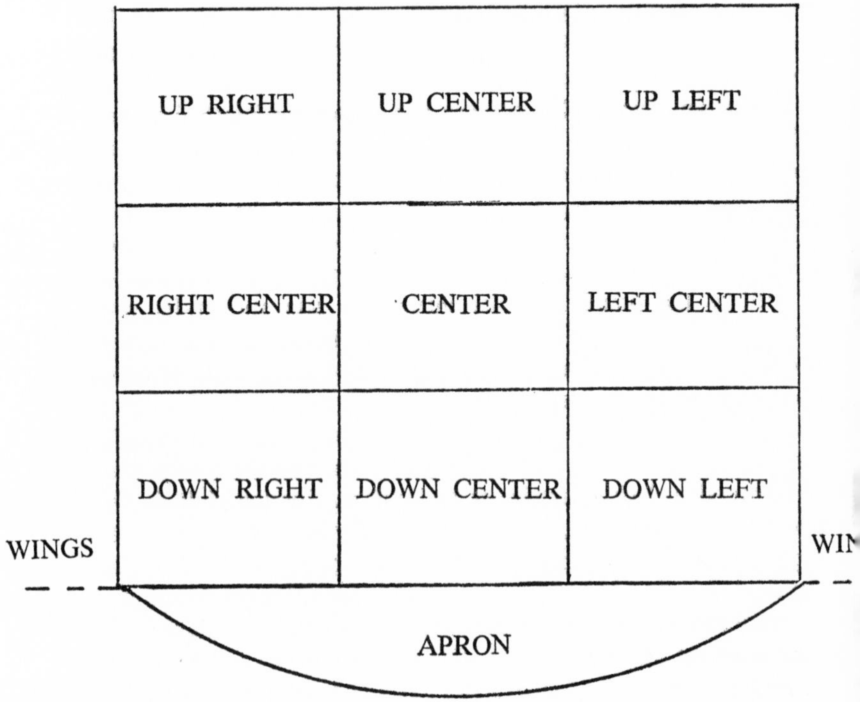

UP RIGHT	UP CENTER	UP LEFT
RIGHT CENTER	CENTER	LEFT CENTER
DOWN RIGHT	DOWN CENTER	DOWN LEFT

WINGS

WIN

APRON

picture of the set, but rather a careful diagram of the floor area, which indicates where each piece of scenery will be placed, its relative size, and the space left on the stage for easy movement. He will be careful to put entrances where the actors can use them most comfortably and effectively. Although he will probably not have the scenery available much before final rehearsals, he will try to find pieces of comparable size so that the cast becomes used to the plan and will have as little trouble as possible adjusting to the setting when it appears.

The director will also want to list all pieces of scenery so that he can check them off as he collects or makes them. The beginner will find that the simpler the setting, the fewer the problems and, incidentally, the more effective the stage will probably be.

THE STAGE MANAGER

This is an important job, and one that a responsible boy or girl can do and enjoy. He should be appointed at the same time the cast is selected and given a script of his own. He attends all scheduled rehearsals and keeps a record of all cuts, action, and business. It is a good idea for him to sit at one side of the stage where he can not only see and hear but call the actors for their entrances.

Under most circumstances, he will be able to pull the curtains and handle or give cues for the lights. He works closely with the director, and assumes as much authority as the director feels he can when the play is presented. The stage manager has a chance to grow in his job, for he is important to every aspect of the production and learns, by doing, the meaning of the word, "responsibility."

CASTING THE PLAY

This preliminary work done, the director is now ready to give his attention to casting the play. In creative dramatics, the cast changes with every playing. In the formal production, however, there is one cast that rehearses each scene a number of times in preparation for a public performance. The matter of casting is, therefore, important. The director tries to get the best possible cast together, and usually does it by means of tryouts. He is obligated to do a certain amount of type-casting. For example, a giant must be played by a very large boy; a dwarf, or elf, by a child who is small; a princess, by a girl who is unusually attractive. To cast for any other reason than theatrical effectiveness is a questionable practice.

The audience must believe in the reality of the characters, and if they are too obviously different from the description or implications in the script, an audience cannot find them acceptable. Likewise, the players will feel uncomfortable if they realize that they are not believable, and so the good that the experience may do them is negated by their own feelings of inadequacy. This, of course, is one of the arguments against public performance. An actor cannot grow if he is constantly cast in the same type of role; yet he cannot experiment with a part, for which he is conspicuously miscast, in front of an audience.

Casting should be done carefully, for a mistake made in the beginning may be fatal later. Some directors like to have two casts. This is a good idea, provided there is sufficient time for a double set of rehearsals. It is a precaution against illness and accidents, and gives the entire group a feeling of security. It also provides twice as many opportunities for participation, and should work out well, if there is time enough to rehearse both groups equally. It goes without saying that both casts should have a chance to perform.

STAGE MOVEMENT

Stage movement is the movement of actors about the stage. The director who plots it in advance will find that he saves valuable time in rehearsal. Writing notations in his script, or even making diagrams, will help him see at a glance where the various characters are. Although most published scripts have action included, it seldom works, for the simple reason that no two stages are alike. For example, an important entrance, which the script indicates should be from the right, may have to be reversed if the wing space in the school auditorium cannot accommodate it.

If the movement is memorized along with the lines, and not changed, it is an advantage. Once the general movement is set, the cast is free to develop appropriate business (action) and work on characterization. Early memorization of lines also helps the group move ahead, giving attention to the rhythm of the play, the building of climaxes, projection of voice, and general polishing. Perfection is never the aim when working with children, but their satisfaction will certainly be greater if they can feel well prepared, comfortable, and able to enter into the performance with a sense of security. Encouragement, plus necessary constructive criticism, helps to make the rehearsal period one of pleasure and learning.

SCENERY

Scenery means the large pieces that suggest the locale of the play. There is always controversy as to the difference between scenery and "props." Scenery is background, whereas properties are those items used by the actors.

The trend today (and a fortunate trend it is for inexperienced and young groups) is toward curtains, rather than box sets, and suggested, rather than realistic settings. For example, a bench, a table, chairs, stools, perhaps a fireplace, or a hutch—if available—will suggest a peasant's cottage, without the necessity of building flats, putting in doors, or painting an elaborate representational background. Some of the most effective settings, both on Broadway and off, have been abstract, or so simple as to focus all the attention on the play and the players.

Platforms and steps are helpful in creating different levels, thus adding variety in appearance and making for interesting movement. A bright tablecloth, a few large flowers, two or three benches or stools can often provide all that is needed. Children have wonderfully imaginative ideas for suggesting scenery; what they do need is practical help in constructing it, and supporting the pieces. If the director works closely with the art department of the school, most of the backstage problems can easily be solved. And, best of all, the stage crew or scenery committee will have an ideal opportunity to learn techniques of painting and handling materials.

Scenery is usually not needed until the final rehearsals. It is suggested that if it can be ready a week in advance of the first dress rehearsal, the players will have a chance to get used to it, and not have to add that adjustment to costumes and other last minute details. A few *do*'s and *don't*'s may be helpful:

1. Scenery should enhance, not distract.
2. Scenery should be firm, not flimsy.
3. Scenery should unify the production.
4. Scenery should be in keeping with the mood of the play.
5. Scenery should suggest the time and place of the story and the circumstances of the characters.
6. Scenery and costumes should be planned together.
7. Scenery should help the players, not get in their way.

PROPERTIES

Very little needs to be said about properties. They are all the objects (usually small) used by the players. If the school has a property closet, many commonly-used items can be kept and brought out when needed. Baskets, canes, wooden bowls, china, swords, and the like, are basic equipment. Some things must be borrowed, some made. It is a challenge to the ingenuity of the committee when, for example, such things as a "golden goose," a "snow man," a "roast chicken," or a "birthday cake" are called for. Papier-mâché and *Styrofoam* are excellent materials for the unusual item, but, again, the young or inexperienced committee needs help in construction.

One other word regarding props: the property committee learns what responsibility is all about, for objects are often needed at particular moments in the play, and the absence of them can ruin an otherwise excellent scene. Properties should be checked before and after every rehearsal and performance, and, if damaged or missing, replaced. It is a good idea to begin gathering the properties as soon as the play goes into rehearsal so as to give the actors ample time to get used to handling them.

COSTUMES

Costumes, like scenery, can be a source of worry and frustration to the teacher whose group is too young or inexperienced to assume responsibility for them. Sometimes parents take a hand with the costumes, and sometimes the art department offers assistance. The former may be a satisfactory arrangement, but all too often it builds what should have been a simple performance into a major production. Too much emphasis is put on the mounting, and the public performance with adult contributions takes precedence over the learning of roles. The second arrangement—assistance from the art department—is decidedly preferable, since it keeps the play within the framework of the school, and may give the class an opportunity to help design or even make some part of the costumes. If neither type of cooperation is available, the teacher should try to solve the matter of clothing by merely suggesting it, or adapting easily obtainable garments to the play.

For example, aprons, hats, vests, capes, boots, and shawls are easily come by and go a long way toward suggesting various kinds of characters. Children accept simple suggestions readily, and do not demand complete or authentic outfits. Blue jeans, tights, and colored T-shirts are in the wardrobes of most children and young people today, regardless of economic circumstances. If these can be chosen with a color scheme in mind, they can be used as costumes for many folk tales, or plays with historical backgrounds.

Paper, and paper cambric—a material that has been used widely—should be avoided. Paper tears easily, and so is hazardous. Cambric comes in raw colors, is stiff, and unsatisfactory to wear. Its popularity has probably been the result of its cheapness, but it would seem better to do without costumes, if the budget is limited, than to use materials that are hard to handle and ineffective. Muslin, percale, and corduroy are far better, if costumes are to be made. They look well on the stage and are much more lasting. It is further suggested that all good costumes, whether made for a particular occasion or given to the school, be saved and kept in good repair. The collection of basic garments should be a continuing project; as time goes on, it will provide many, sometimes all, of the costumes needed for future productions.

It is generally better not to put old and authentic garments and inexpensive, newly-made costumes on the stage at the same time. The effect is usually that of making the old look faded and dirty and the new—cheap, and too bright. Occasionally, the two can be combined, but, in general, it is better to use one or the other for a unified overall impression.

Here, also, a few suggestions are offered as to the function of costumes:

1. Costumes should suggest the personality, age, occupation, and financial circumstances of the characters.
2. Costumes should belong to the period and setting of the play.
3. Costumes should be appropriate to the season of the year, as suggested by the story.
4. Costumes should help to unify the production.
5. Costumes should be planned with the scenery in mind; they should carry out the color scheme and look well against the background.
6. Costumes should not distract for reasons of brightness, richness, or design, unless, of course, there is a reason for it.
7. Costumes should fit the wearers and be clean and well pressed.
8. Costumes should be secure, neither carelessly made nor too fragile to be safe.
9. Costumes should make the wearers feel appropriately dressed and comfortable, not self-conscious.

REHEARSALS

In the beginning, the director, regardless of the group, will have many decisions to make and many details to organize. Once he has cast the play, decided upon the floor plan, and has made arrangements for settings and costumes, he can get down to the serious business of rehearsing. It was stated earlier that time spent on improvisation will be time well spent; the cast will become thoroughly acquainted with the characters and the plot.

He is now ready to set up a rehearsal schedule. It is hoped that, for the teacher or director of children, this will be an informal procedure. Even though a performance date has been set, and the work planned, he must try to avoid the anxiety and boredom that mar rehearsals of so many non-professional productions. For this reason, rehearsals should be frequent but short. Scenes, rather than the entire play, should be rehearsed first; complete run-throughs come later.

Early memorization of lines is advocated, since it frees the players to move and develop pertinent business. People memorize at different rates of speed, but the sooner it is done, the more productive the rehearsal periods will become. Most important is probably interpretation. Discussions along the way help the actors to learn who the characters are, and why they behave as they do. Such questions as these should be answered:

1. How would you describe the character you are playing?
2. What is his motivation?
3. How does he relate to others?
4. What are his individual qualities? (Personality, temperament, age, occupation, background, likes, dislikes, education, beliefs.)

Blocking the scenes comes next. If the director plans movement in advance, he will be able to approach a rehearsal, knowing when characters enter and leave, by what door, and where they sit or stand. It is a good idea to note all movements on a master script. Often, when a few days have passed between rehearsals, there is disagreement as to what was done before. A careful record will answer the questions so that the rehearsal can proceed.

Business, which is individual action in keeping with the character, can be developed next. For example, knitting, sweeping, eating, etc., add to the reality of the characters and give young players something definite to do. The more times business is repeated, the more natural it becomes. As was mentioned earlier, if properties are available at the beginning of the rehearsal period, the players grow used to them, and can handle them with ease and naturalness.

Composition, or "stage picture," is another thing for the director to bear in mind. Even an experienced actor cannot see the grouping on the stage when he is part of it; hence the director, who is watching closely from the front, must be aware of the composition. Are the players hiding each other? Can important business be seen? Are entrances blocked? If there are several players together, do they make a pleasing picture? Does one composition flow into another? All of this pertains much more to the play designed for an outside audience; yet, even under the most informal circumstances, it is important that the players be clearly seen and heard. Blocking can put the players at a disadvantage and prevent important action from being observed.

If dances or songs are included, they should be rehearsed and integrated as early as possible. It is always a temptation to let them go, but the director will find that this makes for a weak spot, or a slow transition. Such business should appear to spring from the play and belong to it; it should not be imposed for the purpose of adding more people, or relieving monotony. If a player is absent, the stage manager or another person should step into the part. When the director reads the lines from out front, the cast is at a disadvantage; for, while the lines are delivered, the space is empty, and the scene very often breaks down. This is another good reason for double casting. It assures each group of a substitute at a moment's notice.

As the rehearsal period proceeds, the play should grow in feeling, understanding, technical competence, and unity. Smoothness will come as lines are learned, the business perfected, and the actors develop rapport with each other. Rough spots should be ironed out in the beginning, rather than left to the end for polishing. And, finally, if the director can maintain a spirit of fun, the rehearsal period will be a source of pleasure as the cast shares the satisfaction of building something together.

As in creative dramatics, the director occasonally finds a show-off, or clown, in the cast. He does not want to inhibit inventiveness but he cannot afford byplay, which disrupts the rehearsal and takes the attention away from the script. Clowning must be stopped at once, for it can jeopardize the entire performance. Most children and young people, if approached constructively, will see that practical and private joking are out of order and, for the good of the production, their energy must be used to build, not break up, a scene.

Teamwork is both a necessity to a good performance and a deep satisfaction to the players. There is probably no experience comparable to the comradery that develops during rehearsals. A special feeling binds a group together when it shares the hard work, the creative effort, the interdependence, and the fun of rehearsing and presenting a play.

THE DRESS REHEARSAL

The dress rehearsal can be either a horrendous experience or a satisfying culmination of weeks of group effort. When details have been well planned, and the scenery and costumes are ready, there is no reason why it should not be the high point of the rehearsal period. The old adage, "a poor dress rehearsal makes a good show," is fallacious. It is true to a degree only when the dress rehearsal is so bad that the cast makes one last mighty effort to prevent the play from being a disaster. This always involves work that should have been done weeks before; with this work completed, the cast is ready to add the final details with a sense of security.

Two, or even three, dress rehearsals are desirable, and should be planned from the beginning. At the first one, the scenery should be finished and in place. At the second and third, costumes should be worn, so that by the time the play goes on, the cast and backstage crew have mastered all of the problems. After each dress rehearsal and performance, costumes should be hung up carefully and properties checked. This not only helps to keep things in good order but instills a sense of responsibility in the players. Even in the most informal of plays, the actors should remain backstage and not mingle with the audience. Food and other refreshments have no place in a dressing room. They are a risk to the costumes, and divert the players.

If makeup is used (and with children it seems unnecessary), it should be tried out first for effectiveness. Again, makeup extends or enhances a character; it does not create one. Sometimes a player will say, "I'll be all right when I'm made up and get into my costume." He will be better, perhaps, but if he has not succeeded in creating a character by that time, costumes and makeup cannot do it for him.

If there is a curtain call, it should be rehearsed so that the players are ready to come out and take a bow to the audience. One curtain call is sufficient for the audience to show its appreciation. Although there is some difference of opinion about this, the curtain call is a convention of the formal theatre, and an audience should be given a chance to observe it.

THE PERFORMANCE

Once again, let it be stated that a performance by beginners, or children, should be simple and informal. The director has the greatest responsibility here, for his attitude of calm encouragement will be contagious. If he regards the play as a good piece of work, which the cast and crew take pleasure in sharing, they will view it in much the same way. They will look forward to the performance with anticipation rather than anxiety. Both excessive criticism and excessive praise are as harmful at this stage as at any other. The most satisfying response a group can be accorded is the honest enjoyment of the audience. They will know that they have succeeded in achieving their goal: successful communication.

THE AUDITORIUM

One aspect of producing a play that is frequently overlooked is that of the auditorium. Ushers may be members of the class, who have worked on committees and so are free when the dress rehearsals are over. Ushering is an excellent way for them to perform a necessary function. If there are programs, they may hand them out, though in an informal situation, a narrator is a preferred way of imparting necessary information to the audience.

Attendance should be by invitation only, rather than by ticket. When tickets are sold, there is an added emphasis on perfection, and a felt obligation to make elaborate settings and costumes. Young players feel the strain, and the "sharing" too often turns into "showing." Publicity, also, should be restricted to posters made by the group, and oral announcements. The greater the participation of the class in every aspect of the production and the fewer contributions from outside, the more positive values the experience will have.

SUMMARY

To summarize: the presentation of a play for an audience should be done only when older children are involved, and then, infrequently. Informality and simplicity should be stressed if the basic values of communication and sharing are to be realized. There is real difference of opinion as to whether children should ever appear before an audience, for fear of destroying their spontaneity and naturalness. This is a valid argument, but the contention here is that performance will probably do no harm if it is done without pressure, thus avoiding drudgery. The teacher must become director, supplying showmanship, and making certain decisions. As teacher, however, she tries to involve every member of the group so that the procedure is as democratic as possible.

In the school, club, or camp play, the educational and social values come first. The product will hold interest for the viewers if they are properly oriented, and their appreciation is the natural consequence of a successful attempt at communication. If these emphases are preserved, the leader and group will find producing a play a richly rewarding experience. There is probably nothing that binds a group together more closely than the production of a play; and no joy more lasting than the memory of a play, in which all the contributions of all the participants have dovetailed so well that each has had a share in its success.

CHAPTER 10

In Conclusion

PIONEERING PROGRAMS

The preceding chapters have dealt with creative dramatics as part of a curriculum, or, at least, an art to be included, whenever time and curriculum permit. Mention has been made of camp or club use, and perhaps a word more should be said on this subject, since drama is a popular activity in the recreation program, and a field in which, at the present time, the demand for qualified leaders exceeds the supply. Some outstanding work has been done in settlement houses and community centers since the early part of the century, and much continues to go on in this area today. Indeed, the first recognition of drama as an educational and social tool came from such centers as the Educational Alliance, the Henry Street Settlement, Christadora House, and Greenwich House in New York; Hull House in Chicago; Goodrich House, and the Karamu Theatre in Cleveland. Many other settlements, from Boston to the West Coast, included classes in storytelling and informal dramatics under the guidance of social workers and the Junior League.

The little theatre movement of the twenties brought similar activities to the children of other communities, but it was not until the forties that the major responsibility was assumed by educational institutions. Notable for its pioneering efforts in this field since 1925 has been Northwestern University, which, in cooperation with the public schools of Evanston, under the distinguished leadership of Winifred Ward, has demonstrated what town and gown can do, working together. There have been other ventures, too numerous to mention, some of which have resulted in permanent programs, contributing both to the children of the community and the training of teachers. Well known among these are Adelphi University, Johns Hopkins University, Michigan State University, Mills College of Education, National College of Education, San Francisco

State College, Southern Illinois University, Teachers College of Columbia University, the University of Denver, the University of Kansas, the University of Minnesota, the University of Utah, and the University of Washington. Many other colleges and universities offer work as either a curricular inclusion or an extracurricular activity, with a touring program or campus performances of plays for children's audiences.

Libraries and playgrounds have introduced drama to some communities, and individual teachers, particularly in the private schools, have made valuable contributions. The Children's Theatre Conference, first established in 1944 as a committee dedicated to the promotion of children's theatre and creative dramatics, became a full-fledged division of the American Educational Theatre Association in 1951. Its membership, interestingly enough, has always included teachers and leaders from universities, colleges and schools, community theatres, settlement houses, the Association of Junior Leagues of America, the professional theatre, and interested citizenry. Annual conventions, held every August, provide programs demonstrating work done in the various regions of the country, as well as talks, symposia, and panel discussions on topics of current interest. Workshops in creative dramatics and puppetry, under the direction of outstanding leaders, have often been planned prior to the opening of the conference, in response to the members' demand for further training. While the principal interest at the present time appears to be the introduction of creative dramatics into the school curriculum, there is a growing enthusiasm for its inclusion in camp, hospital, and special education programs. Reports on research in the field indicate the effectiveness of this aspect of drama as a social and educational technique.

CREATIVE DRAMATICS IN THE CAMP PROGRAM

Except for the arts camps, dramatics is rarely one of the more important activities of the camp program. Camps exist primarily to give city children an experience in group living in an outdoor setting. An opportunity to engage in a variety of sports is provided, with nature study, music, arts and crafts, and dramatics, as well as other activities from which to choose. Because of this emphasis, children should not be expected to spend long hours indoors, in rehearsals, but rather to enjoy dramatics and share the results of their work in occasional informal programs. Creative dramatics is, therefore, an ideal form of theatre for campers of all ages and backgrounds. Pantomime, improvisation, and simple, out-of-door pageantry can contribute both to the participants and to those occasions when the group comes together for programs. Full production with scenery and costumes would seem to have no place in the average camp; the drama counselor might better prepare herself by studying creative dramatics techniques so that she is able to work informally with campers of all ages, rather than formally for an audience. Rehearsals, or working periods, should be short and flexible; this, however, does not mean that time should be wasted or misspent. No activity brings satisfaction unless it is looked upon with respect; hence, informal dramatics, seriously undertaken, has as much to offer the camp as it has the community center, or school.

AN EXPERIMENT IN TRAINING

One reportedly successful experiment in creative dramatics training was carried out in a workshop for teachers held at a mountain camp in Switzerland. A leader with twenty-five participants (all kindergarten and elementary school teachers) lived and worked together for a week. The members of the group did not know each other beforehand, but became well acquainted through the close association of informal classes, discussion groups, and meals taken together in the dining hall. The first classes were conducted in a large room, bare except for a carpet on the floor and a piano. Participants wore informal clothing and soft shoes, or rhythm sandals. On the first morning, they were asked to walk around, to get used to the space they would work in. Movement and rhythms followed, with piano accompaniment. Next came simple exercises in pantomime.

The Grimm tale of *Frau Holle* was introduced the next day, but for several sessions only portions of the story were played. The leader then took the group outdoors and had them try the scenes in the woods under the trees. In pairs they enacted the scene of Frau Holle's trying to pull the girl into the cottage. This was followed by the scene in the doorway with the shower of gold, and the dripping of tar. By the end of the week, they had played the entire story outdoors, in a setting appropriate to the tale and conducive to physical freedom.

Mornings began with singing, movement, and dance. Evenings included the readings from modern literature, and group discussion. These, and Bible stories, were enacted by the participants so that they had the experience of approaching material as children might, but making ultimate use of literary works that challenged them on an adult level. According to one member of the group, the greatest values of the workshop were the sense of freedom it engendered, the loss of self-consciousness that ensued, and the concept of creative dramatics as an art form, which emerged by the end of the week. This illustration is cited because of the unusual opportunity it offered for group work in a simple yet ideal setting. While the camp program is filled with a variety of different activities, it does offer the same advantages of plenty of space, an outdoor setting, and freedom from the usual daily distractions.[1]

WORKSHOPS AND TRAINING

Many workshops in creative dramatics are held in the United States each year under a variety of sponsorships. Some are part of the summer school offerings of universities and colleges. Others are sponsored by such organizations as the Children's Theatre Conference (both national and regional), the Association for Childhood Education International, the National Recreation Association, and the National Catholic Theatre Conference. Still others are among the in-service courses for public school teachers, held after school, or on Saturdays. The Junior League, women's clubs, religious and recreational organizations, the Headstart Program, as well as individual community theatres and churches, have instituted programs

---

1. Fraulein Brigitt Streuli, 2 Hauptlehrerin, Kantonales Kindergartnerinnen, Semenar, Brugg Aargau, Switzerland.

for the training of their drama leaders. Surveys have been made from time to time in an effort to determine the amount and kind of training that is being offered by educational institutions throughout the country, but it would be difficult to list or assess the numbers and types of workshops that are conducted by the other institutions and organizations mentioned. It is significant, however, that they seem to be on the increase, and that hundreds of teachers and leaders take part in them each year for the purpose of broadening their own backgrounds and adding another dimension to their programs.

Most successful seem to be the workshops that include demonstration, actual work with children, and participation in acting on the adult level. Reading, lectures, and discussion are to be taken for granted, but practical laboratory experience is essential for any study of the arts. It has been this leader's experience that the members most reluctant to participate in the beginning have always mentioned it first when evaluating the course. Only a concentrated workshop, or a semester's class, permits enough hours to include all of these activities. The acquisition of fine technical skills should not be expected, for techniques are a developmental process, attained over a much longer period of time spent in practice and study.

THE TEACHER OR LEADER

With so much expressed interest in creative dramatics, is it not appropriate to raise some questions regarding the teacher? What special qualifications should he have? What kind of education best prepares him to teach creative dramatics? Is a pure theatre background a disadvantage? Is a workshop experience sufficient preparation? Dare the teacher embark on a program of his own without some specialized training?

Without discrediting academic preparation, what seems most important are those personal attributes that make him, first of all, a good teacher. If he already possesses the qualities of sympathetic leadership, imagination, and respect for the ideas of others, he has the basic requirements. His sensitivity to the individuals in his class is necessary to an activity that is participant-centered, with the growth of each child an objective. In other words, although he is teaching an art and should therefore have some knowledge and appreciation of it as a form, a genuine concern for the players is of equal importance.

The successful creative dramatics teacher guides rather than directs. He is able to work with others, offering and accepting ideas. To him, sharing is more important than showing; thus his satisfaction will come through the process as well as from the product. When he does show the work of his group, he will be clear as to what is demonstration and what is performance. Unless he is working with groups over the age of twelve, he will avoid the latter, in favor of informal class demonstrations.

The teacher of creative dramatics finds his own way. No methods courses can prepare him perfectly, for no two groups are alike. What works well with one class does not work with another. Materials and methods that arouse a response in one group may be totally inadequate in a second, whose cultural background and experiences are different. Knowledge of the neighborhood in which he is working is just as important as a knowledge of literature and drama. He must find out for himself what stimulates and what fails to elicit a response. Familiarity with techniques is an invaluable asset, but the imaginative leader will create his own methods.

A sense of humor helps him over those periods when nothing goes right. His ability to laugh with the group, as well as at himself, enables him to carry on, in spite of failures and frustrations. Because he is interested in all kinds of things, he will have an expanding background of information on which to draw. He learns constantly from his pupils. He must also learn not to expect good results each time the class meets. Many of the efforts will be pedestrian and disappointing, but, as Hughes Mearns points out: "Those who work with children creatively are compelled to discard or ignore a hundred attempts while they are getting a mere half-dozen good ones." [2] It is these "good ones" that inspire others, and encourage the leader to keep on trying.

---

2. Hughes Mearns, *op. cit.*, p. 33.

He maintains high standards, knowing that what he accepts in the beginning is what they are capable of at the time, but that he can expect more from them later. By establishing an atmosphere in which all feel important, he will challenge his class to give only their best; the teacher waits for this, without demanding or pushing. For this reason, it is often more difficult to teach creative dramatics than formal drama. The absence of a basic structure, or script, demands flexibility, judgment, a willingness to accept the efforts of the shy and inarticulate, patience, and the confidence that something of value is forthcoming. This is not easy for the teacher whose only previous experience has been with the formal play, or whose theatre background has conditioned him to expect technically perfect results within a stipulated period of time.

The teacher must, at the same time, set limits. The establishment of boundaries does not limit freedom, but, rather, gives a sense of security to the young or inexperienced player. As in any class, discipline must be maintained at all times in order to ensure, for each member, the freedom to experiment. In his book, *Child Drama,* Peter Slade has observed that "The manner of handling is what matters, and, because of this, some of the best work with children is done by experienced teachers who really understand what they are doing and yet, strangely enough, have very little knowledge of drama."[3]

All of this is not meant to imply that specialized training is unnecessary; what is meant is that the successful teacher of creative dramatics seems to possess certain attitudes and qualities of personality that distinguish and qualify him. A background that includes both education and theatre is ideal, but the interested leader, whatever his preparation, may acquire, through course work and reading, additional information and techniques. Classroom teachers, professional actors, and social workers have all achieved notable results. Because of their belief that creative dramatics has a contribution to make, they have adapted their own individual skills to its use, with intelligence and imagination.

---

3. Peter Slade, *op. cit.*, p. 271.

SUMMARY

In conclusion, creative dramatics may be viewed as a way of learning, a means of self-expression, or an art form in which many learnings are possible. Viewed as the last, these learnings include self-knowledge, a knowledge of others, and intellectual development.

Self-Knowledge

Through drama, the player thinks, plans, and organizes. He feels deeply but learns to channel and control his emotions. His communication skills are involved as he speaks and expresses his ideas. Through rhythms and physical movement, he makes use of his body. Working with others teaches him the meaning of cooperation.

Knowledge of Others

By trying on characters, he learns about other people. Playing a variety of parts helps him to think and feel like persons different from himself. Being part of a group not only teaches him something of teamwork but sensitizes him to the feelings of those with whom he is working. And, finally, through the material the teacher brings in, he is exposed to other peoples' customs, to ideas and values that may be foreign to his own.

Intellectual Development

Play has long been recognized by nursery educators as experimentation that offers unlimited possibilities for learning. Recently, Jean Piaget has written extensively on the function of play in the intellectual development of young children. He sees conceptual thinking as originating in spontaneous play through manipulation of objects and social collaboration with other children. Recent research indicates that an appropriate balance between spontaneous and more structured play is desirable.[4] No activity provides a greater variety of opportunities for learning than creative dramatics, regardless of the level.

CONCLUSION

A basic requirement of any activity is that it be a satisfying experience for both leader and group. The more successful the project, the greater the degree of satisfaction. As the leader grows in experience, he will recognize the possibilities in a variety of materials and methods, and his group will likewise grow in security and the ability to tackle problems more imaginatively. This is true of the leader and his group on any age level, whether in a school or recreational setting.

Through the spread of our mass media, we have become known as a "spectator society." Participation in any of the arts is, therefore, more needed today than at any other period in our history. Drama, of all the arts, demands of the practitioner a total involvement. By offering an opportunity for participation in drama, we are helping to preserve something of the play impulse in all of its joy, freedom, and order.

> High is our calling, friend! Creative art
> Demands the service of a mind and heart!
>
> Wordsworth

---

4. Millie Almay, "Spontaneous Play: An Avenue for Intellectual Development." Reprint from *The Bulletin of the Institute of Child Study,* University of Toronto, Volume 28, Number 2, 1966.

A Selected Bibliography

ON CREATIVE DRAMATICS AND CHILDREN'S THEATRE

ALLSTROM, ELIZABETH, *Let's Play a Story* (New York: The Friendship Press, 1957).

This is a handbook on the uses of informal dramatization as an educational tool for teachers and leaders. The author offers practical suggestions on story-playing, choral speaking, rhythms, puppets, festivals, and simple productions. It is brief but useful to the inexperienced teacher of young children.

ANDREWS, GLADYS, *Creative Rhythmic Movement for Children* (New York: Prentice Hall, Inc., 1954).

Although this book has been used widely for a number of years, it remains one of the most useful in the teaching of rhythms and dramatic play. Often used as a text, it is an excellent addition to any library of creative dramatics material.

BROWN, CORRINE, *Creative Drama in the Lower School* (New York: Appleton-Century-Crofts, Inc., 1929).

One of the first books on the subject to appear, this is still one of the clearest and best for the classroom teacher. As the title states, it is directed toward the lower grades. There is more emphasis on producing plays for audiences than is found in many of the other books on the subject.

BURGER, ISABELLE, *Creative Play Acting* (New York: A. S. Barnes & Co., Inc., 1950).

This is a practical book written by a leader of long and wide experience. It includes many practical exercises and techniques for acting and movement.

CROSSCUP, RICHARD, *Children and Dramatics* (New York: Charles Scribner's Sons, 1966).

A recent addition to the literature in the field, Mr. Crosscup's book is an autobiographical account of his twenty-seven years' experience in one school. Of greatest value is the view he gives of a gifted teacher, able to stimulate the creativity of his pupils. Social values are stressed.

DAVIS, JED, and MARY ANN WATKINS, *Children's Theatre* (New York: Harper and Row, Inc., 1961).

An outstanding and practical book on formal theatre. Because it is concerned with production and production techniques, it will be of greatest interest to teachers of older children, or adult students who are presenting plays for young audiences and are, therefore, looking for expert and detailed guidance.

DURLAND, FRANCES, *Creative Dramatics for Children* (Yellow Springs, Ohio: The Antioch Press, 1952).

A good and clear presentation of the way in which a creative play is developed.

FITZGERALD, BURDETTE, *Let's Act the Story* (Palo Alto, California: Fearon Publishers, Inc., 1957).

This is a handbook for the beginner. It is concise but authoritative. Written by an experienced practitioner in the field, it offers valuable suggestions for creative acting.

FITZGERALD, BURDETTE, *World Tales for Creative Dramatics and Storytelling* (New York: Prentice-Hall, Inc., 1962).

In this collection, the author introduces a wide variety of stories not usually found in collections of this sort. She has drawn from the folklore of countries rarely represented in anthologies of children's literature, thus making an interesting contribution to the field.

HAAGA, AGNES, and PATRICIA RANDLES, *Supplementary Material for Use in Creative Dramatics with Younger Children* (Seattle: University of Washington Press, 1952).

This outline of lessons, planned and evaluated by the authors, is of great practical value to teachers of younger children. It is unique in describing the activities of each session in detail, the music and literature used, and the children's reactions.

KASE, ROBERT, *Stories for Creative Acting* (New York: Samuel French, Inc., 1961).

Professor Kase has collected stories recommended to him by experts in the field. All of the stories have been used with success, thus making this a valuable addition to any teacher's library.

KERMAN, GERTRUDE, *Plays and Creative Ways with Children* (Irvington-on-Hudson, New York: Harvey House, Inc., 1961).

This is a handsome volume in which the author, an experienced teacher, describes how she has worked with children in the dramatization of stories.

LEASE, RUTH, and GERALDINE BRAIN SIKS, *Creative Dramatics for Home, School and Community* (New York: Harper and Row, 1952).

A popular book that does exactly what the title promises. It tells how a teacher, recreation leader, or parent may work with children to help develop imagination and creativity.

LOWNDES, POLLY, *Creative Assemblies* (Minneapolis: T. S. Denison and Company, Inc., 1961).

This book is an outgrowth of the author's years as a teacher of creative dramatics in junior high school. It is addressed to the classroom teacher, and describes how imaginative assembly programs may be developed. It should be extremely helpful to teachers of older children.

SIKS, GERALDINE BRAIN, *Creative Dramatics, An Art for Children* (New York: Harper and Row, 1960).

This book has been used widely as a text since its publication in 1960. Written by an expert, it discusses the characteristics of children of different age levels and material appropriate for them. It is filled with illustrations and anecdotes which add human interest and aid in clarifying her points.

SIKS, GERALDINE BRAIN, ed., *Children's Theatre and Creative Dramatics: Principles and Practices* (Seattle: University of Washington Press, 1961).

This volume, edited by Geraldine Siks, was written by a group of experts on the various aspects of children's theatre and creative dramatics. It contains much factual information, which should have its greatest value for the student who wishes to become generally informed on the subject.

SIKS, GERALDINE BRAIN, *Children's Literature for Dramatization* (New York: Harper and Row, 1964).

A collection of stories and poems, old and new, for the classroom teacher and group leader. The introductions to the stories make it particularly valuable to less experienced teachers but it is enormously useful to anyone working in the field.

SLADE, PETER, *Child Drama* (London: University of London Press, 1954).

Written by an expert in children's dramatics in England, this lengthy book presents a philosophy and way of working. It is detailed and informative, and should be of interest to all leaders and teachers of creative dramatics. The author takes an unequivocal stand against public performance for children under twelve.

TAYLOR, LOREN E., *Storytelling and Dramatization* (Minneapolis: Burgess Publishing Company, 1965).

This book is exactly what the title indicates. It should find its greatest usefulness among classroom teachers seeking help in the presentation of material to children, as well as guiding them in handling it dramatically.

WALKER, PAMELA, *Seven Steps to Creative Children's Dramatics* (New York: Hill and Wang, Inc., 1957).

This book outlines certain specific steps in teaching acting to children. The author is clear and concise, and her approach provides clear guidelines for the teacher of creative dramatics who is thinking in terms of more formal presentation.

WARD, WINIFRED, *Playmaking with Children* (New York: Appleton-Century-Crofts, Inc., 1957).

This book, by a distinguished leader in the field, has been widely used as a college text. It is arranged both as to age levels and use, including dramatics in school, recreation, religious education, and therapy. Highly readable, it is valuable both for the beginning and the experienced teacher.

WARD, WINIFRED, *Stories to Dramatize* (Anchorage, Kentucky: The Anchorage Press, 1952).

In this collection, the author has included a rich variety of stories, and some poems, for use in school and recreation groups. It is arranged for children on various age levels (from six to fourteen) and contains material that the author has tested and found rewarding in her many years of experience.

WARD, WINIFRED, *Theatre for Children* (Anchorage, Kentucky: The Anchorage Press, 1958).

Theatre for Children deals exclusively with formal theatre: material, techniques, values. It is designed for directors of plays for child audiences and, as such, covers the subject with thoroughness and authority.

A SELECTED LIST OF BOOKS ON CHORAL SPEAKING

ABNEY, LOUISE, *Choral Speaking Arrangements for the Lower Grades* (Boston: The Expression Company, 1937).

GULLAN, MARJORIE, *The Speech Choir* (New York: Harper and Row, 1937).

HUCKLEBERRY, ALAN W., and EDWARD S. STROTHER, *Speech Education for the Elementary Teacher* (Boston: Allyn & Bacon, Inc., 1966, Chapter VI).

RASMUSSEN, CARRIE, *Choral Speaking for Speech Improvement* (Boston: The Expression Company, 1942).

RASMUSSEN, CARRIE, *Let's Say Poetry Together and Have Fun* (Minneapolis: Burgess Publishing Company, 1962).

RASMUSSEN, CARRIE, *Poems for Play Time* (Boston: The Expression Company, 1942).

WHITE, ALICEN, *A Bouquet of Poems* (East Orange, New Jersey: The Triad Publishing Company, 1966).

TEACHING AND THE RELATED ARTS

BATCHELDER, MARJORIE, and VIRGINIA LEE COMER, *Puppets and Plays: A Creative Approach* (New York: Harper and Row, Inc., 1956).

COLE, NATALIE R., *The Arts in the Classroom* (New York: The John Day Company, Inc., 1940).

HARTLEY, RUTH, LAWRENCE FRANK, and ROBERT GOLDENSON, *Understanding Children's Play* (New York: Columbia University Press, 1964).

LINDERMAN, EARL W., and DONALD W. HERBERHOLZ, *Developing Artistic and Perceptual Awareness* (Dubuque: William C. Brown Company, 1964).

LOWENFELD, VIKTOR, *Creative and Mental Growth,* Third Edition (New York: The Macmillan Company, 1949).

MEARNS, HUGHES, *Creative Power,* Second Revised Edition (New York: Dover Publications, Inc., 1958).

MIEL, ALICE, *Creativity in Teaching* (New York: Wadsworth Publishing Company, 1961).

PAMPHLETS

ASSOCIATION FOR CHILDHOOD EDUCATION INTERNATIONAL, *Creative Dramatics,* (Washington, D. C.: Association for Childhood Education International, 1961).

WARD, WINIFRED, *Drama With and For Children,* United States Department of Health, Education and Welfare, Bulletin #30 (Washington, D.C.: Government Printing Office, 1960).

SOME 16-MM. FILMS FOR USE IN TEACHING DRAMATICS AND PUPPETRY

ABC of Puppets (2 parts)

10 min. sd. b/w or color

Bailey Film Service ($5.00)
6509 De Longpre Avenue
Hollywood, California 90028

University of Michigan ($4.25)
A-V Center
Frieze Building
720 E. Huron Street
Ann Arbor, Michigan

A-V Center ($3.25 each part)
Division of University Relations
Florida State University
Tallahassee, Florida 32306

Part One: This film shows the making and dressing of simple hand puppets, using inexpensive, easily obtained materials.

Part Two: In this film more elaborate puppets of papier-mâché and wire are shown. A simple play produced by children illustrates the use of these puppets in performance.

Creative Dramatics: The First Steps

29 min. sd. color

Northwestern Film Library ($10.00)
614 Davis Street
Evanston, Illinois

This is an outstanding film that demonstrates the teaching of creative dramatics to a group of fourth-grade children. Guided by an experienced teacher, the group moves from the faltering first steps to the creation of a drama.

Ideas and Me

17 min. sd. color

Dallas Theatre Center ($6.00)
3636 Turtle Creek Blvd.
Dallas, Texas 75219

Children are shown participating in creative theatre. Growth and personal development are emphasized in this film.

Marcel Marceau Pantomimes

13 min. sd. color

Brandon Films, Inc ($15.00)
200 W. 57th Street
New York, New York 10019

Marcel Marceau is shown in three of his best-known works: *David and Goliath, The Lion Tamer,* and *Butterfly Chase.* The film serves both as entertainment and demonstration of the artist's technique.

Pantomime

21 min. sil. b/w

Dallas Theatre Center ($4.00)
3636 Turtle Creek Blvd.
Dallas, Texas 75219

Classic mime and modern dance techniques are included in this film designed for teaching.

Play Fair

15 min. sd. color

A-V Service ($3.25)
University of Washington
Seattle, Washington 91805

This is a report in film made at the University of Washington. It shows a children's creative dramatics festival presented by the School of Drama.

Puppets—Creative Work and Play

16 min. sd. b/w

Bureau of A-V Instruction ($3.00)
Extension Division
State University of Iowa
Iowa City, Iowa 55240

This film shows school children being given instruction in how to make and operate puppets.

Showtime

22 min. sd. b/w

A-V Service ($3.65)
University of Illinois
Division of University Extension
704 S. Sixth Street
Champaign, Illinois 61820

Bureau of A-V Instruction (Apply)
University of Wisconsin
Extension Division
1312 W. Johnson Street
Madison, Wisconsin 54306

This film follows the production of a play from beginning to final rehearsals and performance. Clubs, classes, and teachers who direct dramatic activities with older groups will find it of particular interest.

Story Acting Is Fun

10 min. sd. b/w

A-V Center ($2.25)
Division of University Relations
Florida State University
Tallahassee, Florida 32306

This film is designed to aid the development of social and language skills. It shows the acting out of everyday experiences as well as stories and poems.

The Unborn

30 min. sd. b/w

Associated Film Consultants, Inc. (Apply)
501 Madison Avenue
New York, New York 10022

This is an original screenplay produced in documentary style. The dialogue came from the players, and the situations are based on their own experiences. It is both moving as a creative work and effective in showing the results of the creative process.

Index